HIND SWARAJ AND SATYAGRAHA

HIND SWARAJ AND SATYAGRAHA

Ramjee Singh

Commonwealth

Hind Swaraj and Satyagraha

Edition : 2027

ISBN 978-81-311-0305-0

Published by :
COMMONWEALTH PUBLISHERS PVT. LTD.
4831/24, Prahlad Street,
Ansari Road, Darya Ganj,
New Delhi - 110002
Ph. : 23272541, 23257835
Fax : 91- 011- 23257835
e-mail : commonwealthbooks@gmail.com

Laser Typesetting by :
Dimple Computers
Delhi

Printed at :
Roshan Offset Printers
Delhi

Preface

Hind Swaraj was written in 1909 by Mahatma Gandhi on the board of a ship on his return journey from London to South Africa. It was because of an intensive Psychological and spiritual thirst arising out of his soul. Hence, it is not nearly and abstract Philosophical work like Plato's Republic, nor Thomas moor's Utopia nor Windel Wilke's 'One world' or Rahul Sanskritayana's novel called Baishwi Sadi . In fact, Hind Swaraj is therefore is not a book of recreation or wishful thinking, but a book of action. It is simply descriptive but also prescriptive.

The nearest comparison to Hind Swaraj is the Communist Manifesto written jointly by Marx and Engle in 1848. In back-ground of capitalistic exploitation of poor peasants and factory workers. The native feudalism and neo-Colonialism were in the back ground of Both Marx and Gandhi. By Marxian analysis is based on Economic interpretation of History and Dialectical Materialism, Gandhi Presence a comprehensive and holistic outlook. According to Gandhi life is a unity. It is not a like water-tite compartment. Hence Life is not only economics but also cultural and spirituality. True man cannot live without bread but it is also true that he can not live with bread alone. In short Materialism can hardly offer incentive to higher values.

Hence Hind Swaraj is Critique of modern materialistic and hedonistic civilization.

Both Marx and Gandhi are prophets of social change. But while according to Marx force is the mid-wife of change with the result that he does not avoid or discard violence social changes, Gandhi invents a moral equivalent of war and struggle, called Satyagrah. In the modern world having a Leviathan—like state power. Empowered with greater power of destruction, Satyagrah has greater scope for a successful and lasting change-both internal and External.

Hence Communist Manifesto is was relevant for the 20th Century. Hind Swaraj is most appropriates Manifesto for the 21st Century.

Ramjee Singh

Contents

1

Introducing the Hind Swaraj

Background Statement

No book has been more misunderstood in modern times than Gandhi's Hind Swaraj (1909) which was prescribed by the then Government of India as soon it was issued as booklet (24 March, 1910). To some it is anti-science, anti-progress and even anti-civilization, while to others it contains the ideas of a new world-order and something out of the tune with the course of socio-economic and political evaluation of human society. While some dub the book as a sociological dyophia and as reaction against dehumanisation and alienation of man in modern technological culture, while others, acclaimed it as superior to Rosseau's Social Contract and Karl Mark's Das Capital. On the whole the book appealed to all those European authors (GDH Cole, Fredrick Sody, C.D. Burns, John Middleton Mury, JD Brestford, Hugh Fausset, Elaude Hougton, Gerald Heard, Irene Rathbone) who even expected their doubts on many of Gandhi's Formulation.

Hind Swaraj, as a whole theory of life has aroused varying reactions among different sections, both western and India. It was manifesto of a new civilization, rooted in materialism. Hence Middleton Murry acclaimed the book as one of the spiritual classics of the world and the greatest that has been written in modern times. As a matter of practical service to the present conditions of India, "Gandhi's gospel will be of any more value than was the same gospel preached by Gautama to India" (T.D. Brestford). Agreeing with the concern of Gandhi to growing mechanisation, Hugh Fausset regarded it as one of the best modern hand books of the revolution which must happen to us all if we are to fulfil the creative purpose of life. However many regarded Gandhian prescriptions as simply impracticable, that various problems like unemployment population growth, food shortage etc. could not be solved without resort to industrialisation.

Some regard Gandhi's attitude as illogical, unreasonable and unhistorical, which had vitiated all his conclusions and recommendations. There are also those who are willing to incorporate some of the policies but were opposed to implement them.

It is all the more necessary to study this Gandhian classic with a free mind and in the perspective of new findings. H.S. has a pivotal position in his writings and has been aptly held by Mahadev Desai as 'Seminal'.

2

Concept of Swaraj in Gandhi's Thought : A Critical Appraisal

Gandhi considered self-realization to be the ultimate aim of man's life and service of humanity to be the only way for its achievements. In order to ensure the speedy realization of this objective, he sought to adumberate the features of a well-ordered society. He found modern civilization, to be more precise, western civilization to short of ideal society of his conception. It was against this civilization that Gandhi wanted to establish an order which should be egalitarian, non-exploitative, non-violent and peaceful in structure. It was to be the society of future, which Gandhi aimed at. He called it by the name of *Swaraj*.

Concept of Swaraj is not of recent origin but it became very popular during the freedom movement when 'Swaraj' was on the lips of every Indian. A book written during those days draws the picture of Swaraj in these words, "Swaraj is the dream of a poetic mind, the mirage of a dry intellectual, the gossamer—thread of a philosopher, spinning his ideas, the incessant topic of street discussion, the ban and anathema to be the committee—harnessed school master, the apple of discord in debating clubs, the object of laughter in many of our bar—associations and the golden apple guarded by the sleepless eyes of non-corporation."[1] It meant so many things to so many persons—absolute, unqualified independence, Dominion self government, a system of political make shifts, Dharam-Rajya, world federation etc. In the words of

Chittaranjan Das, "Swaraj is vedantic freedom of soul in the universe of free community of souls."[2]

Swaraj is a vedic term which literally means rule over one's own self and its original connotation meant autonomy of the moral self where strict control is exercised over the senses. Swaraj first acquired its political meaning at the hands of Dadabhai Naoroji and later on, it was popularised by Bal Gangadhar Tilak[3], Sri Aurobindo[4], Annie Besant and many others. But the concept of Swaraj as conceived by Gandhi is the most important one as it was Gandhi who first give a mass-orientation to the concept of Swaraj. In fact the whole Swaraj movement was shaped by the forceful yet dynamic personality of Mahatma Gandhi, whose-record of sacrifice, suffering, idealistic faith, hard common sense and comprehension of Indian masses was an unbeaten record and whose religious directness of speech and action is a constant enigma to the alien mind obsessed by long generations of political diplomacy.

Gandhi for the first time, enunciated his ideal of Swaraj in 'Hind Swaraj' (1909). He seized upon a traditional religious notion of Swaraj and transformed it into a meaningful part of the technique which was to operate not for the individual salvation alone but also with in the sphere of social polity. He defined the term Swaraj as a condition "When we learn to rule ourselves". He observed in Hind Swaraj that real home rule is self control. Again in Young India dated 19.3.31 he said, "Swaraj is a sacred word meaning self-rule and self-restraint and not freedom from all restraints which independence often means" through out his life, Gandhi insisted on this subjective aspect of freedom for it was an article of faith for him. He wrote in 1920, "Govt. over self is the truest 'Swaraj', it is synonymous with *Moksha* or salvation"[5] and, "For me, movement of Swaraj is a movement of self-purification."[6]

Gandhi's Swaraj contains two fold usage; one is for individual *i.e.* personal Swaraj and the other for the collective aggregate of individuals in society *i.e.* National Swaraj. He laid more stress on the individual aspect of Swaraj as for him, individual is the basic indivisible unit of Swaraj. First condition he laid down for personal Swaraj is control over lust. According to Gandhi, self-rule is an impossibility without conquering the lust with in ourselves. Rule over all without rule over self is deceptive and disappointing. Personal Swaraj implies that there will be minimum rule by the govt. and the society and individual will rule over himself in such a manner that he will not be an obstacle in the way of others. Rather he shall serve others to the maximum of his capacity. Gandhi's concept of Swaraj is first step towards the attainment of *Ram-Rajya*. In it all the individuals would achieve maximum degree of self-rule which would be guided by certain ideals and principles.

National Swaraj, according to Gandhi, is mere an aggregation of Swaraj of individuals. To quote Gandhi, "Swaraj of a people means sum-total of the Swaraj of individuals."[7] He elaborated the same idea while saying, "Self government depends upon our own internal strength, upon our ability to fight against the heaviest odds. Indeed, self-govt. which does not require that continuous striving to attain it and sustain it is not worth the name. I have therefore endeavoured to show both in word and deed that political self-government that is self-govt. for a large number of men and women—is no better than individual self-govt. and therefore it is to be attained by precisely the same means that are required for individual self-govt. and self-rule."[8] Thus national Swaraj according to Gandhi is national self-rule and self-restraint in political, economic social and religious spheres. To quote him, "let there be no mistake about my conception of Swaraj. It is complete independence of alien control and complete economic independence so at one end, you have political independence and at the other economic. It has two more ends. One of them is moral and social, the corresponding end is Dharma, *i.e.* religion in the highest sense of the term...... Let us call this the square of Swaraj which will be out of shape if any of its angles is untrue."[9]

Politically, Swaraj means that the people of the country must have complete control over all political institutions and "A state such that we can maintain our separate existence without the presence of English. If it is to be a partnership, it must be a partnership at will." He said, "By Swaraj I mean govt. of India by the consent of people as ascertained by the largest no. of population, male or female, native born or domiciled, who have contributed by the manual labour to the service of the state and have taken the trouble of having registered their names as voters."[10] Swaraj can be attained when we are capable of resisting the abuse of authority and it is only possible when our masses are educated to resist and control it. Gandhian Swaraj is a democratic and decentralized state in which ultimate authority will be vested with the people and even smallest will enjoy the freedom without any political and social and economic disability. In order to underline the principle of decentralization, Gandhi gave the slogan of 'back to the villages'. Under Plato's inspiration, he maintained that every village will become a self sufficient republic—a complete republic, independent of its neighbours for its own vital demands...' Village Panchayat will play the role of primary unit of political power. No political domination either by individual or by group would be there. The benefits of this self-rule will be enjoyed by the different sections of society in common without any discrimination.

In economic terminology, his Swaraj has "but one meaning eradication of poverty from India and men and women will have enough clothing.., and enough food also. In fact, such a state will be free from economic exploitation ensuring economic equality."[11] For Gandhi, economic equality is the master key to Swaraj. His economic Swaraj has socialist content also as it aim at ameliorating the conditions of workers and peasants but on the lines of humanitarian & moral socialism. Unlike Marxian socialism, Gandhian socialism believes in non-violent and peaceful transformation of society. He also stood for freedom from British Capitalists and capital as also their

Indian counterpart. He presented trusteeship as an alternative to the drawbacks of western capitalism. His socialism is, in short, moral, egalitarian, democratic, decentralized, individualistic and also non-violent. Bread-labour and Khadi are the core of Gandhian economics. He accepted the use of machinery in industries to the extent a physician may use poison to treat the patient. He was against heavy industries and advocated production by the masses in place of mass-production. For the purpose he was in favour of preserving cottage industries.

Social and moral aspect of Gandhi's Swaraj implies regard for interests of others. Swaraj won through non-violent struggle self-purification would also solve the problems of minorities in India. Swaraj can never be achieved by crushing the rights of any community big or small but by ensuring even-handed justice and fair treatment to all including the poorest and the weakest in the land. In Gandhi's own words "Swaraj is to be for all including the maimed, the blind, the starving toiling millions." This Swaraj will not be a rule of majority on the other hand, it will be a rule of justice. There will be no untouchability, no communal riots and tensions. Women would have an equal status in Swaraj. Reformist mind in Gandhi ruled out the possibilities of armed forces in Swaraj state. It will rather be defended by non-violent Satyagrahis.

Fourth aspect of the square of Gandhian Swaraj is *Dharma* *i.e.* spiritual Swaraj. He wrote, "what I want to achieve—what I have been striving and pinning to achieve these thirty years—is self realization, to see God face to face, to attain *Moksha*. I live and move and have my goal in the pursuit of this goal. All this I do by the way of speaking and writing, and all my ventures in the political field are directed to the same end."[12] Spiritual Swaraj, according to Gandhi, can be achieved only after the achievement of first three as it is based on the duties that each individual has to perform towards his society. *Dharma*, to Gandhi, did not mean sectarianism but the science of morals. His religion is universal and not limited to Hinduism only but it is above religions and transcends all.

Thoughts, words and deeds that an individual finds necessary in order to realize his self, constitute religion according to Gandhi.

Thus, achievement of total Swaraj is based upon four pillars of the square which embraces each and every aspect of individual and social life.

Gandhi has often been labelled as an idealist whose ideals are mere wishful thinking and they have no relevance in modern world as human beings have their limits too. They can never achieve perfection. So is said about his concept of Swaraj which is called a utopia—beyond realization while Tilak and Aurobindo are considered to be more practical in their interpretations of Swaraj. But Gandhi's prophecies made decades ago about industrialization and machinery, since and technology, population and about many other social and economic problems have become true. It shows the far sightedness and practical vision of Gandhi and shows the way for establishment of Swaraj which can be a solution to many of today's problems. The basic questions which arise regarding Swaraj are—Has Gandhian view of Swaraj been defined by the others in the same way as it was conceived by Gandhi? Which factors were responsible in shaping his philosophy of Swaraj? After 45 years of independence we have not been able to establish Swaraj despite its inclusion in the Indian Constitution as a goal to be attained in the form of Directive Principles of State Policy. What reasons can be traced for our failure to realize it? Is it a Utopia? If not, what steps can be taken for its implementation? Modern democratic state has not been able to fulfil the very purpose for which state comes into being—*Sarvodya* and alround development of individual. In this case, can Swaraj be an appropriate alternative to the failure of present system? Concept of Swaraj which also includes self sufficiency in principle is contrary to international trade & commerce and it can cause tensions in international relations. Then can it be possible to establish peace and harmony between nations with the realisation of Swaraj!

Purpose of the Study

Purpose of this study is to examine the true nature and meaning of Swaraj as conceived by Gandhi and to enquire and explore the possibilities for its implementation.

Review of the Existing Literature

There is a good deal of literature available on Gandhi's life and thoughts—Political, Economic and Social etc. But there is hardly any work which is entirely devoted to the study of Swaraj. S.H. Patil's book *Gandhi and Swaraj* has tried to present a total picture of Gandhian Swaraj. All the four aspect of the square of Swaraj *i.e.* Political, Economic, Social and religious have been dealt with in this book. But things have not been discussed in detail and only a few pages of the book have been devoted to the political aspect.

Besides, some books have relatively dealt with the subject.

Buddhadeva Bhattacharyya's book *Evolution of Political Philosophy of Mahatma Gandhi* evaluates Gandhi's political ideas from an objective and a critical point of view. Last chapter of the book 'political theory' contains some material on Swaraj but the subject has been taken up mainly from political point of view.

In Raghwan Iyer's book *Moral and Political writings of Mahatma Gandhi* (Non-violent Resistence and Social Transformation—Vol. III) which contains essential and selected writings from collected works of Mahatma Gandhi issue of Swaraj has been taken up. But again, things have not been discussed in detail. Thorough study of economic, social and political aspects has been neglected.

Ramashray Roy's book *Self & Society* is a good treatise on Gandhi's vision of desirable society. Despite its concentration on Gandhi's critique of modern civilization, his vision of self & society, relationship between individual and society and in the last his view of freedom has been discussed. But notion of Swaraj, its meaning essential conditions and provisions in Swaraj State as laid down by Gandhi are not found in the book.

Hind-Swaraj : A Fresh Look, edited by Nageshwar Prasad contains articles and discussion on *Hind Swaraj*. But Gandhi's view of Swaraj does not come up directly for discussion.

In short, none of the existing material has discussed Gandhi's view of Swaraj in totality nor has examined its relevance in modern times.

Research Methodology & Sources

As far as methodology is concerned, it will basically be a library work. Research will mainly depend upon primary sources. Secondary sources will, however, be consulted whenever necessary. The former includes—the *Collected Works of Mahatma Gandhi*, Journals edited by him—*Young India and Harijan* and Gandhi's own writings. The latter includes the books written by others (as mentioned in the bibliography).

Chapterization

Tentative chapter plan of the research design is as follows :

CHAPTER I—PROBLEM AND MEANING

In this chapter, the origin of the term, its meaning in general and its growth from Vedas to today will be discussed. This chapter will discuss Swaraj as conceived by others like Tilak, Aurobindo and Gandhi etc.

CHAPTER II—PHILOSOPHY OF SWARAJ

Gandhi's concept of Swaraj is based on his Philosophy of life. According to him, the ultimate aim of human life is self-realization. In this chapter, philosophy of Swaraj—Swaraj as a moral and spiritual aspect will be discussed.

CHAPTER III—POLITICAL ASPECT OF SWARAJ

Gandhian Swaraj is democratic and decentralized in which

authority is vested with the people and each village is economically self-supporting and politically autonomous. This chapter will discuss the provisions made by Gandhi in the political set-up of Swaraj State.

CHAPTER IV—SWARAJ AS AN ECONOMIC CONCEPT

Gandhi was aware of the fact that political self-govt. without economic self-sufficiency is just a myth. In this chapter, Gandhi's economic views regarding Swaraj will be discussed.

CHAPTER V—SWARAJ—ITS SOCIAL ASPECT

According to Gandhi, Swaraj of society is a sum-total of the Swaraj of individuals. He wanted to establish a stable society based upon certain principles like love, non-violence, truth and equality. In this chapter social aspect of Gandhian and Swaraj will be discussed.

CHAPTER VI—SUMMING UP

Diwakar, R.R., *My Encounter with Gandhi* (New Delhi : Gandhi Peace Foundation), 1989.

Dutta, D.K., *Moral and Political Philosophy of Mahatma Gandhi* : A Critical Analysis (New Delhi : Intellectual Publishing House), 1980.

Fisher, Louis, *The Life of Mahatma Gandhi* (New York : Harper & Brothers), 1950.

Gandhi Ji on Rural Development (New Delhi : Ministry of Education And Broadcasting) n.d.

Ganguli, B.N., *Gandhi's Social Philosophy : Perspective and Relevance* (Delhi : Vikas Publishing House), 1973.

Hick, John & Hemple, Lamout C; (eds.) *Gandhi's Significance Today* (Houndmills : MacMillan Co.), 1989.

Iyer, Raghwan, *Moral and Political Writings of Mahatma Gandhi,* III Vols. (Oxford : Claredon Press), 1987.

Kappen, Mercy (ed.), *Gandhi And Social Action Today* (New Delhi : Vikas Publishing House), 1990.

Karunakaran, K.P., *Indian Politics from Dadabhai Naoroji to Mahatma Gandhi : A Study of Political Ideas of Modern India* (New Delhi : Geetanjali Publishing), 1988.

Kriplani, J.B., *Gandhi : His Life & Thought* (New Delhi : Publications Division, Ministry of Information & Broadcasting, Govt. of India), 1970.

Varma, Vishwa Nath Prasad, *Political Philosophy of Mahatma Gandhi & Sarvodya* (Agra : K. Lakshmi Narayan Aggarwal), 1965.

Vinoba, *Swaraj Sastra* (Varanasi : Sarva Seva Sangh Prakashan), 1973.

Wadhwa, Madhuri, *Gandhi between Tradition & Modernity* (New Delhi : Deep & Deep Publications), 1991.

REFERENCES

1. Nripendra Chandra Banerji, The Ideal of Swaraj (Madras : Ganesh & Co.), 1921, p. 47.
2. *Ibid.*, p. 48.
3. For details, see *Bal Gangadhar Tilak* (Madrass G.A. Natesan & Co.) 1918.
4. For details, see Sri Aurobindo—Thoughts & Aphormisms (Pondicheri : Sri Aurobindo Ashram), 1959.
5. *Young India*, December 8, 1920, p. 886.
6. *Young India*, June, 12, 1924, p. 195.
7. *Harijan*, March 25, 1939, p. 64.
8. *Young India*, March 19, 1931, p. 38.
9. *Harijan*, January 2, 1937, p. 374.
10. *The Collected Works of Mahatma Gandhi*, Vol. XXVI, p. 50.
11. *Harijan*, January 2, 1937, p.
12. Quoted from J.K. Mehta, *Gandhian Thought : An Analytical Study* (New Delhi : Ashish Publishing House), 1985.

3

Gandhi's Weltanshaung in Hind Swaraj

No book has been more misunderstood in modern time as Gandhi's *Hind Swaraj*.[1] To some it is anti-science, anti-civilisation and anti-machinery, while others dub it as sociological dystopian vision created as a reaction against dehumanisation and alienation of man in modern technological culture. This is because Hind Swaraj is read bereft of its weltanshaung.

Life is unity. It cannot be divided into watertight compartments called social, political and religious. All act and react upon one another.[2] There is no dichotomy between the spiritual and the temporal. The spiritual saw expresses itself only through the ordinary activities of life.[3] Hence no line can be drawn between the different compartments. One's everyday life was never capable or being separated from his spiritual being.[4] Gandhi's world view was, therefore, inclusive and based on a dynamic concept of civilization which is amply reflected in his philosophy of history. Convention history to Gandhi was worse than useless, for it is merely a chronicle of the doings of kings and emperors", a 'record of the wars of the world', " a record of every interruption of the even working of the force of love or of the soul.[5] Hence the real history of mankind should concern the changes in man and his nature, society and its functions, the meaning of civilisation, and the progress of man along the steep and narrow spiritual path.[6] He believed that the sum total of the energy of mankind is not to bring us down but to lift us up and that is the result of the definite, if unconscious working of the law of love. Human society is a ceaseless growth, an unfoldment in terms of spirituality.[7] Nothing in this world is static, everything is kinetic. If there is no progression, then there is inevitable regression.[8] However, Gandhi thinks that inspite of temporary set backs, the human race is on the whole marching forwards. Man has already been steadily progressing towards *ahimsa*. From cannibalism, man became a wandering hunter and from a nomad he settled down to a civilised life. All these are signs of progressive *ahimsa* and diminishing *himsa*.[9] Life persists in the midst of destruction and therefore there must be a higher law than that of destruction. On the whole, history can be made to show a change for the better in human nature when a sufficiently long view is taken of things. The observed progress in human history has been brought about by the operation of intelligent love.

All life in its essence is one and the humans are working consciously or unconsciously towards the realisation of that identity.[10] That is the experience of God. Gandhi is a God intoxicated man. Gandhi minus God is zero. According to Gandhi, without Him (God) not a blade of grass moves. Whilst everything around us is ever changing, every dying, there is underlying all that change is a living power that is changeless.[11] "The substance of conventional history is "name and forms" matter little, they come and go. That which is permanent eludes the historian of events. Truth transcends history.[12] Therefore, for Gandhi, God is Truth, may, Truth is God. Where Gandhi speaks of God or Truth, the Marxian speaks of History or of Nature.

But neither God nor Truth, deflect a Gandhi from *man*. Man is not God but neither he is different from the rays of God. He is a special creation of God and is distinct from the rest. Hence, to Gandhi, "the individual is the one supreme consideration."[13] He has faith in the essential goodness of human nature. However, there is always a conflict going on between man's spirit and the Devil in his body but ultimately the good are never destroyed. Man's destined purpose is to conquer old habits, to overcome the evil in him and to restore the good to its rightful place. Man cannot be at peace with himself till he has become like unto God.[14] The true history of man, therefore, is to be seen in his ceaseless striving to be with God, to be good because God is not only Truth but also Good and Beautiful, benevolent and Love. Like the individual, history of human society is ripen with a two fold conflict but ultimately it is an unfoldment in terms of spirituality. Conventional history does not reveal all man's potentialities. If we are to make progress we must not repeat history but make new history, of which man is quite capable of because of his soul—force or force of love, which is the same as the force or soul or truth.[15] Real historical progress "pertain to progress in the inner being of man rather than an extension of power over nature or other human beings or territories."[16] It has to reveal man's progress or regress in terms of morality. It has cosmic overtones for Gandhi because in the womb of history lies embedded the spirit of the cosmic man. Hence Gandhian view of history and human nature is that of hope and triumph. It is the saga of man's striving after the supreme or the unfoldment of his own spirituality. This is precisely the reason that Gandhi, in many of his historical generalisations about modern civilization, he seems to be hyper critical to the extent he is supposed to have betrayed an unhistorical trait. According to Gandhi, the acid test of condemnation or admiration of any civilization lies in its ethical and spiritual worth. If Gandhi was 'anti' to anything at all. He was not anti-science and anti-civilization but anti-pride, anti-selfishness and anti-vice because those are all anti-man.[17] Man is superior to the system.[18] Swaraj lies in the individual. The individual is the one supreme consideration.[19] Man is the measure of all-political and social organization, educational and cultural system, technological scientific progress. Technology is not and end in itself. It is only a means to man's happiness and progress. However, modern technology is not merely a means for increasing production and reducing costs. It raised not only complex technical and economic problems but also social, psychological and cultural issues of deep import.[20] In the 19th century, Christian and romantic writers and the so-called utopian socialists a constantly protested against the evils of unbridled industrialism. The bulk of the current sociological and psychological literature is a 'crisis literature' preoccupied with the theme of social disintegration and psychoneurotic disorder resulting from the growth of an over-centralised, over-mechanised industrial structure.[21] The universe reveals a purpose outside the temporal side or human affairs. Man, though he may be falliable and fallen, is much more than a machine.[22] Men have been entirely divorced from the world or nature.[23] This forced attunement of the human organism to the rigid and unnatural routines of the city, the factory and the machine has produced chronic, nerve shattering tensions. There has been loss of permanent contact with natural elements, natural beings and rhythms has blunted and bifurcated sensibility,[24] causing a weakening of the feeling of human presence as it was felt and lived in the natural environment.[25] Masses of men have been hudled into hideous overcrowded cities like "cages of human spirit", which is a "pathological phenomena"[26] the fountain source or divitalisation and delinquency. Hence R.N. Fox's personal solution lies in getting as "far away from machine industry (as I could), to cease being a tool of mass production and endeavour to become a human being again.[27] The Report of the "Study of Conference on Human Problems of Industrial Communities, [28] presided over by the Duke of Edinburg came to the conclusion that industry was not an end in itself. In fact, material advancement does not necessarily mean moral progress. Hence writing about the ideas and teachings of Gandhi's Hind Swaraj says— "Gandhiji's case against the West looks, then, infinitely stronger than it looked to us Westerners, thirty years ago.[29] Hence, Mr. Hugh is right when he says that "the whole purpose of the book (*Hind Swaraj*) is to save India, not from Englishmen, but from the modern civilization which is eating into the vitals of the West."[30] Modern technics with excessive specilisation have deprived of all spontaneity, creative, aesthetic joy and all personal and human significance. Only a few limbs and a few conditioned reflexes are called into service.[31] Research in a number of factories showed that over 60 percent workers suffered badly from boredom, in the metallurgical industry...90 percent without immediate significance.[32] Mechanisation and automation have reduced man to mere clog in the wheel, where men are corrupted and degraded.[33] The industrialists through the supply of standardized ready made amusements make us mechanical imbecile in our leisure. A UNESCO study complains of the lack of community satisfaction in modern culture.[34] The signs of very great individual unhappiness suicide, mental illness, dejection, divorce, delinquency and anti-social activities, etc. are legion. The price of progress[35] as cited by F. Juenger is too great for its results in a neurotic society. Modern technism, Centralism appears to be inherent sociological tendency of industrial growth involving a great sacrifice of human values. Modern technics is applicable only in man production and hence it a capital costs are very high. It is a phase in material progress, but only a phase, destined to be superseded when its a development has become sufficiently complete.[36] The Crisis in European culture is clear. Those who were impressed by successes are now disillustioned by failure.[37] It is rash to judge the success or failure of a culture in the light of one or two centuries, being human existence at least two millions years old. Political and economic efficiency should not be regarded as the sole criterion or culture. It may be that twentieth century will see our technological civilization end by its own devices in a might shambles.[38] Sehumacher re-echoes justice Brandic's lamentation on the qualities of temporary life and dun the curse of bigness.[39] Mechanics and techniques have become a source of idolatory. Man today is a slave of machine. Slavery dehumanises man from with resulting in the loss of mediative, the creative and the spiritual enrichment.[40] Writing about "Work in Western Civilization", M. Ludovice exposes the hallowness by saying that sooner or latter we shall have to acknowledge that our civilization was born of *forced labour* and reared upon it, and try to devise a *way or life* from which all the features depending on Forced Labour will have been eliminated. "The alternative is a Police State, in which the *dictator* or *dictators* wield the power to drive people to uncongenical labours by means of severs sanctions and their attending cruelties."[41] Technology has precipitated a revolution in man communication, and the combination of the totalitarian monopoly of mass media and the rise of mass literacy has opened up opportunities of indoctrination without parallel in the past.[42] The refinement of technology have enabled the rulers to perfect and project their controls over the whole range of social life. Technology has influenced social consciousness as well as economic and social structure of society. While it has infused the spirit of calculation pushing into the background the power of irrational forces, it has generated a tendency towards large-scale industry and organisation, the decline in the skilled labour, the rise of entrepreneurs and creation of a commercial system. It has also resulted in transformation in social structure such as conflict between entrepreneurs, capitalists and workers, difficulty in equitable distribution, rise in the class of technocrats and bureaucratisation. Modern technology has made human labour more monstrous. The lower classes have been emancipated. Older classical educational ideals were shattered and the destruction of all values of a liberal society followed.[43] We find the Frankenstien of modern technology with the horrors of war and technological unemployment.[44] Last but not the least, the industrial hazards like industrial diseases, poison and accidents represent a social loss of considerable magnitude measured in terms of pain, loss of life, loss of earning capacity, loss of restoration and disturbance of economic efficiency. It is impossible to sum up the emotional loss. Thus industrial hazards represent to society a dead loss of considerable magnitude.[45] Machine qua machine is madeness and is the source of corruption and decivilisation of modern man. Our social system is full of tension and this is due to contradiction of the system. The cause of all contradiction is centralism in production and in power leading to exploitation and oppression.[46] Then there is a direct link between poverty and exploitation. Gandhi observed in this connection that the world has sufficient things to met the needs of all its inhabitants but not enough to meet the greed of a single person.[47] We need a new design for living. An imitation of the affluent societies with super advanced technology and the accepted notions of economic growth ought to be challenged. The increased productive efficiency and cheapness of the products is offset by the high expenses in finding suitable substitutes for natural resources, by the biological cost and the cost in terms of social unrest, class-conflict, mental ill-health etc. No body bothers about these costs are long term bills and we do not enter into the balance sheet of the money costs of production.[48] Through mechanisation of agriculture, there is *Rape of the Earth* (Jacks and Whyte) degrading the soil to quench our inordinate lust for wealth and power. Then it is the civilization and not the soil that comes to the end. The use of fertilizers may bring bumper crop and vegetables of prize-size but may be deficient in minerals and normal vitamins.

The modern civilization has developed to meet and suit the needs and interests of the greedy and acquisitive person resulting in imbalance in society leading to violence and war. The civilization built upon it becomes a Frankenstein. Random mechanisation of the modes of our living confront us with the dilemma of choosing between man or machine with a tendency towards over-production, modern industrial civilization gives rise to a universal colonial system under which not only a few nations exploit other nations,[49] but also the town exploits the village.[50] Centralisation in politics, it amounts to negation of democracy. A centralised industry based system of economy presents a tempting target to the enemy in times of war and a country with decentralised system of economy can put resistance to the invader much better. Even a Hitler could not devastate seven hundred thousand non-vioent villages.[51]

Technological culture has caused "the devaluation of the human and of man and animal as a source of physical power.[52] This is virtual surrender of human initiative and neglect to the machines. If freedom and creativity are some of the basic values of our being human then indeed science and technology have done serious harm to them.[53] The Sabbath was made for man, not man for the sabbath. Should man live by proxy and machine do everything for him? May I ask then, what remains of life? The result is irritability, discontent and revolt against work. Work is not the anti-thesis of life but a means of realising the full content of life. No doubt we need leisure but a life of all leisure is a life of inferno for the soul of man.[54] Bernard Shaw said—perpetual holiday is the best definition of hell. Arnold Toynbee has shown that easy and luxury has been the most fatal foes of the twenty-seven civilizations which have passed into the oblivion of antiquity.[55] John Galbraith's warning against mad rush for industrialisation is clear:" We have become the slaves of the machine, we have created to serve us and the servitude is felt comfortable as a result of mass suggestion to which consumers are subject."[56] Marcuse's observations are more biting. "The slaves of developed industrial civilizations are sublimated slave, but they are slaves, for slavery is determined."[57] Gandhi therefore pleaded for limiting our indulgences "The mind is a restless bird, the more it gets the more it wants, and still remains unsatisfied. The more we indulge our passions the more unbridled they become.[58] It is unique coincidence that in the land of unheard of affluence, a veritable heaven for plenty, millions of Americans are pursuing lives of voluntary simplicity, would grow from 5 million to 25 million in 1987 and to 60 million in 2000; while those opting for partial voluntary simplicity life styles would grow from 10 million to 35 million in 1987 and 60 million by the turn of the century.[59] Again comes Gandhi : "A man is not necessarily happy because he is rich, or unhappy because he is poor",[60] Fixing up an old house tending to a backyard garden, chopping firewood—more and more young Americans are turning to a lifestyle that makes use of renewable energy-cheap products.[61] Gandhi says that our "ancestors disuaded us from luxuries and pleasures...they further reasoned that large cities were a share and a useless encumbrance and that people would not be happy in them, that there would be gangs of thieves and robbers, prostitution and vice-flourishing in them and that the poor men would be robbed by rich men."[62] The measuring rod of a good civilization is morality—"Kings and their swords were inferior to the sword of ethics—"said Gandhi.[63] Hence, where this cursed modern civilization has not reached, India is happy. The tendency of the Indian civilization is to elevate the moral being, that of the Western civilization is to propagate immortality."[64] Immorality is taught in the name of morality. Ever increasing bodily comforts and luxuries, Fast life, more and more reliances on machinery, instruments of war, Railways, army of Lawyers and Doctors, Parliament and utter disregard for morality and religion constitute the emblems of modern civilization —which is considered a Satanic Civilization according to Mohamed and the Black Age according to Hinduism.[65] Gandhi's attack on machinery is most scatching. According to him, "it is the machinery that has improverished India.[66] Machinery has began to desolate Europe...Machinery is the chief symbol of modern civilization; it represents a great sin.[67] He further said : "If, instead of welcoming machinery as a boon, we should look upon it as an evil, it would ultimately go.[68]

According to Gandhi, the real test of civilization is to raise man to a higher moral level, whereas the haul mark of modern civilization is materialism and selfishness.[69] For example, the railways had only enabled Britain to tighten its hold over India increased frequency of famines, because owing to facility of means of locomotion, people sell out their grain and it is sent to the dearest market; it has spread infectious deiseases, the holy places have become unholy. Evil has got wings hence railways accentuating the evil nature of man.[70] Similarly, according to Gandhi, "the lawyers have enslaved India, have accentuated Hindu-Mohammedan dissension and have confirmed English authority.[71] The profession teaches immorality, as a rule advance quarrels instead of repressing them. The good is due to them as men rather than as lawyers. Their routs; like so many leeches, suck the blood of the poor people.[72] Again, the doctors did positive moral harm to the people by encouraging self-indulgence as they cured people of their diseases caused by their own folly and indulgence. If the doctor had not intervened, nature would have done its work and man would have acquired mastery over himself.[73] Man take less care of their bodies and immorality increases.[74] They sometimes prescribe such medicines which contain either animal fat or spirituous liquor both tabooed by religious sentiments.

In fact, by attacking these emblems of modern civilization Gandhi was diagnosing the causes of moral and spiritual slavery of the Indians. Swaraj is when we learn to rule ourselves.[75] Because we had been thrown off our feet by the strong winds of modern western civilization, we started looking down our cultural heritage, we became imitators of their system-factory-culture, parliamentary system, legal and medical system, etc. and their philosophy of life—materialism and atheism. We have to Indianize ourselves if we want to be free. Slaves ourselves, it would be a mere pretension to think of freeing others.[76] Hence *Hind Swaraj* is not only change of the masters but it is cultural and spiritual freedom of India.

Gandhi's *Hind Swaraj* is a critique of western civilization. It is a manifesto of counter-culture. True he argues his case like a lawyer but we cannot overlook sweeping generalisations regarding the emblems of modern civilizations like machinery parliamentary system, legal and medical professions etc. It seems "a fundamental philosophical error to regard as morally evil any instrument which may be misused. Any mechanism may be misused, but if it is, the moral evil is in the man who misuses it, not in the mechanism."[77] Perhaps the immediate and the urgent blurrs his vision,[78] and he uses crude language. Later on Gandhi trides to rationalise his language and stand by saying that he was not against machinery but the craze for machinery[79] etc. Had he revised the book, several misconceptions would have been removed. But Gandhi did not it even when he was giving a small *message* to the book in 1938. On the other hand, he was a little satisfied that "it stopped that rot that was about to set in among some Indians in south Africa."[80]

While evaluating the book, we must distinguish between the 'essentials' and 'non-essentials'. The core of *Hind Swaraj* lies in the critique of materialism, immoralism and the cult of violence. Civilization means good conduct. It means performance of duty and duty and morality are convertible terms. Spiritual and moral values are the sheet anchor of Indian civilization. Hence, "Indian civilization is the best and that the European is a nine days' wonder."[81] Mr. J.S. Keay, M.P. said that "Indian civilization was not perfunctory, but universal and all-pervading furnishing the country not only with political systems but with social and domestic institutions of the most ramified description."[82] Victor cousin, Maxmuller, Fredrik Von Schlegel, Dubois, J. Young, Thomas Munro, William Wedderbury[83] etc. have given their testimony of the vitality and spirituality of Indian culture.

If 5,00,000 years of developing culture were compressed into 50 years, the entire period of our modern industrial civilization would come about for one day.[84] Hence, any evaluation of modern civilization has to be made with a long-range perspective. The Eco-forum Report (April 1981) of the Stockholm Conference on Environment has proclaimed that "the protection and improvement of the peoples and economic development throughout the world" and is working towards a programme called SURVIVAL 2000.[85] Urban and industrial pollution, soil degradation, destruction of forests; and growing militarization, if not stopped, will change the global climate and cause long-term genetic effects through radiation caused mutations. Hence, in the long march of human progress, sometimes one or two steps back become an ecologic-biological imperatives we have to accept that "man is the source, the centre, and the purpose of all economic and social life. Individual human beings are the should be the foundation, the end, and the subjects of all the institutions in which social life is carried on."[86] The Indian ideal of four fold ends (*Pursarthas*), the cultural and the spiritual forms the highest and the economic the lowest, because the cultural and the spiritual ends in themselves are not pursued for the sake of anything else. According to Hind Swaraj, "this civilization is unquestionably the best."[87] Its beauty lies in its performance and in its ability to survive the shock. Hence, many European genuine have been "Constrained to bend the knee before the East,"[88] where according to Maxmuller "we make our inner life more perfect, more comprehensive, more universal in fact more truly human, a life, not for this life only, but a transfigured and eternal life."[89] So far spiritual knowledge is concerned, according to Schlegel, " Hindustan holds the first rank in point of time."[90] The Indians breathen atmosphere of moral purity.[91] They are true children of natures. Domestic felicity and happiness of married life are matters for emulation. The Indian villages has for centuries remained a bulwork against political disorder, and the home of the simple domestic and social virtues.[92] Gandhi's concept or Swaraj is a concept of purity and perfection formed out of truth, good, and beauty. Hence it is a counterpart of God who is embodiment of purity and perfection, truth, goodness and beauty. Swaraj is the ideal and civilization is the mirror of Swaraj. Science and technology are important forces of civilization but they are means, not end. Neither railways nor hospitals are a test of high and pure civilization. At best they are necessary evil. Neither adds one inch to the moral stature of a nation.[93] Today, our civilization is sick and this sickness owes its origin to us. Gandhi envisages a healthy civilization where there is progress with purity, development with creativity, prosperity with peace of mind. He measured progress in terms of happiness. Hence, he was neither a utilitarian nor an advocate of affluent and materialistic society. He wanted a Sarvodaya society and a Swarajist culture, where we may not be slaves of sensual pleasures. He demonstrated the strength of man's moral values against material ones; and of service and sacrifice as against selfishness and acquisitiveness.

REFERENCES

1. We can refer to some such fictions of our time such as Aldous Huxley's *Brave New World* (1932), *Ape and Essence* (1943), Island (1962), John Wyndham's The *Day of the Triffids* (1951), George Orwell's 1984 (1949); Arthur Koestler's *Darkness at Noon* (1940), Franz Kafka's *In the Penal Settlement* (1919), *Metammorphosis,* Robert Musil's *Der Mann chna Figenschaften*; Pirandello's *Six Characters in Search of an Author*; Ionesco's *Rhinoceros, Becket's waiting for Godot and Endgame* etc.
2. Gandhi, M.K., *Young India,* 2.3.1922.
3. *Ibid.,* 3.0.1925.
4. Gandhi, M.K., *Harijan,* 30.3.1947.
5. Gandhi, M.K., *Hind Swaraj* (Ahmedabad, Navajiwan Publishing House, 1953), p. 78.
6. Gokhale, B.G., "Gandhi and History", *Gandhi Marg* vol. XVIII. 4 Oct. 74, p. 220.
7. Gandhi, M.K., *Young India,* 16.9.1926.
8. Gandhi, M.K., *Harijan,* 11.8.1940.
9. Gandhi, M.K., *Harijan,* 11.8.1940.
10. Gandhi, M.K., *Correspondence with the Govt.,* 1942-44 (Navajiwan 1945), p. 88.
11. Gandhi, M.K., *Young India,* 11.10.1928.
12. Tendulkar, D.B., *Mahatma,* II, 111.
13. Gandhi, M.K., *Harijan,* 11.8.1940.
14. Gandhi, M.K., *Young India,* 10.11.1928.
15. Gandhi, M.K., *Hind Swaraj,* p. 65.
16. Gokhale, B.G., *Ibid.,* p. 225.
17. Mall, N., "Swaraj, Science and Civilization," *Gandhi Marg,* Vol. III No. 6, September 1981, p. 352.
18. Gandhi, M.K., *Young India,* 13.7.1921.
19. *Ibid.,* 13.11.1924.
20. Raj Kishan, *Human Values and Technological Change* (Kashia. B. Sarva Seva Sangha Prakashan, 1958), p. 5.
21. *Ibid.,* pp. 8-9.

22. Rolt, L.T.C., "Science Run Mad", *Aryan Path* (Bombay, March 1956), p. 115.
23. Huxley, Aldous, *Science, Liberty and Peace,* p. 23.
24. Rajkrishna *Ibid.,* p. 9.
25. Friedman, G., "Technological Change and Human Relations", British Journal of Sociology, 1952, pp. 105-107.
26. Ropke W., *Civitas Humana,* pp. 161-162.
27. Fox, R.N., "Machine : Mecca of Moloch", *Aryan Path,* April, 1956, p. 167.
28. "Industrialism and Happiness." Report prepared by J.C. Hunt, *Aryan Path,* October 1956, pp. 438-39.
29. *Ibid.,* p. 439.
30. *Ibid.,* p. 439.
31. Rajkrishna, *Ibid.,* p. 11.
32. Low, A.M., *Science in Industry,* p. 148. Quoted by Rajkrishna, p. 11.
33. Mumford, Lewis, *Condition of Man,* p. 309 (statement attributed to Pope Pius XI).
34. Scott and Lynton, *The Community Factor in Modern Technology,* UNESCO Publications, p. 29-30.
35. Juenger, F., *"The Price of Progress",* Ethics, July, 1952.
36. Coh, G.D.H., "Industrialism", *Encyclopaedia or Social Science* Vol. VIII, p. 18.
37. Dutta, D.M., "The Crisis in European Culture." *Vishwa Bharti,* Feb., 1953, p. 354.
38. Gotshalk, D.M., "Politics and Civilization", *Ethics,* Jan. 1956, p. 86.
39. Morris, Bertram, "Democracy and Culture", *Ethics,* Jan. 1956, p. 89.
40. Paul, Leslie, "The Effect of Technology", *The Hibbert Journal,* October, 1956, pp. 26-33.
41. *Hibbert Journal,* October 1956, p. 34.
42. Paisod, M., "The Challenge of Totalitarianism", *New Leader,* May 7, 1956.

43. Lecerer, Emil, "Technology", *Encyclopaedia of Social Science,* Vol. XIV, pp. 553-557.

44. Ginsberg, B., "Science", *Ibid.,* Vol XIII, p. 602.

45. Rubinow, I.M., "Industrial Hazards", *Encyclopaedia of Social Science,* Vol. VII, p. 702.

46. Handa, Madanlal., "The Existing World Order : A Gandhian Interpretation", *Gandhi Marg,* November 1980, pp. 427-430.

47. Fernandes, Archbishop Angelio, "God's Rule and Man's Role", *Gandhi Marg,* March 1982, p. 699.

48. Pyrelal, *The Last Phase,* Vol II, p. 565.

49. Pyrelal, *Ibid.,* p. 589 "The Economic imperialism of a single tiny island (England) is today keeping the world in chains. If an entire nation of 300 (now 500) millions took to similar economic exploitation, it would strip the world bare like locusts."

50. Mitrany, David, *Marx against the Peasants,* London, 1952.

51. Pandey, S., *The Ultra-Modern Gandhi,* April 1982, p. 22.

52. Heinemann, H., *Existentialism and the Modern Predicament* (New York : 1958), p. 15.

53. Raman, N.S.S., Two Independent Cultures, *Gandhi Marg,* April 1976 p. 87.

54. Pandey, S., "The Ultra-Modern Gandhi", *Gandhi Marg,* April 82, p. 23.

55. *Ibid.,* p. 23.

56. Galbraith, J.K., *The New Industrial State,* p. 19.

57. Marense, L.H., *One Dimensional Man* (London : 1968), p. 32.

58. Gandhi, M.K., *Hind Swaraj,* p. 61.

59. Henderson, C., "Learning to Live Frugally", *SPAN* (NEW YORK), Vol. XX, No. 7, July 1979, p. 14.

60. Gandhi, M.K., *Hind Swaraj,* p. 61.

61. Henderson, C., *Ibid.,* p. 15.

62. Gandhi, M.K., *Hind Swaraj,* pp. 61-62.

63. *Ibid.,* p. 62.

64. *Ibid.,* p. 63.

65. Gandhi, M.K., *Hind Swaraj,* Ch. VI, p. 37.

66. *Ibid.,* p. 93.
67. *Ibid.,* p. 94.
68. *Ibid.,* p. 97.
69. Malhotra, S.L., "Gandhi and the Scientific Outlook", *Gandhi Marg,* April, 1982, p. 46.
70. Gandhi, M.K., *Hind Swaraj,* p. 45.
71. *Ibid.,* p. 54.
72. *Ibid.,* p. 55.
73. *Ibid.,* p. 59.
74. *Ibid.,* p. 59.
75. *Ibid.,* p. 65.
76. *Ibid.,* p. 65.
77. *Ibid.,* p. 7 (Prof. Delisle Burns)
78. *Ibid.,* p. 7 (Middleton Murry)
79. Gandhi, M.K., *Young India,* 13.11.24; 17.6.26; 15.4.26.
80. Gandhi, M.K., *Hind Swaraj,* p. 18.
81. *Ibid.,* p. 101.
82. *Ibid.,* p. 106.
83. *Ibid.,* pp. 106-110.
84. Rob, J.R., "Civilization and Culture", *Encyclopaedia Britannica,* Vol. V., p. 738.
85. "SURVIVAL 2000". Documentations, *Gandhi Marg,* Sept. 1981, p. 367.
86. Fernandes, F., "God's Rule and Man's Role", *Gandhi Marg,* March 1982, p. 695.
87. Gandhi, M.K., *Hind Swaraj,* p. 64
88. *Ibid.,* pp. 106-7, Statement attributed to Victor Cousin.
89. *Ibid.,* 9. 107, Statement attributed to Fredrick Max Muller.
90. *Ibid.,* p. 108, Statement attributed to Fredrick Von Schlegel.
91. *Ibid.,* p. 108, Statement attributed to J. Young.
92. *Ibid.,* p. 110, Statement attributed to Sir William Wedesburn, Bart.
93. *Ibid.,* p. 17, A Word of Explanation.

4

Reconstruction of Gandhi's Hind Swaraj

Birth and Rebirth of Hind Swaraj

Hind Swaraj is like Gandhi's Gospel where he announces his own life-mission. It was written in ten days, between 13 and 22 November 1909, on board the ship *Kildonan Castle* on his return trip from England to South Africa, after what proved to be an abortive lobbying mission for the cause of the South African Indians. It was originally written in Gujarati, his mother tongue. It was so spontaneous and the urge for writing was so strong that writing went on at such a furious pace that when the right hand got tired, he continued with the left hand. He "wrote as if under inspiration".[1] In the entire autograph, only 16 lines have been scratched out and only a few words changed here and there.[2] John Middleton Murry also thinks that *Hind Swaraj* is a "'fundamental document' and it was the outcome of some profound experience of illumination" and in particular, it has a marked affinity in the vehemence of its repudiation of Western civilization with the Discourse road to Viennes.[3] Dr. B.R. Nanda, therefore calls it his "confession of faith."[4]

This small book had a "chequered career". Originally written in Gujarati in 1909, it was serialized in two installments in *Indian Opinion* (Gujarati edition), the weekly published by Gandhi in South Africa. However, in 1910, when it was published as a booklet in India in Gujarati, it was considered as dangerous that the Govt. of India prescribed it along with other publications on the charge that it contained matter declared to be *seditious*.[5] This attracted the notice of some of the Europeans, and also hastened its translation into English in 1910. Gandhian anthologies are vast like an ocean spread into more than one hundred published volumes running into about 50,000 pages. But *Hind Swaraj* is a small booklet of 93 pages (Revised New edition 39, Reprinted 1944, 46, 58, 62, 82 etc.) but it has been regarded as "a very basic document for the study of Gandhi's thought,"[6] or a rather incendiary manifeste."[7] Gandhi himself characterized it as a "whole theory of life" and his most faithful private secretary Mahadeva Desai has aptly called it as *"seminar."*[8] As Anthony Parel has rightly said : "*Hind Swaraj* is the seed from which the tree of Gandhian thought has grown to its full sature.[9] When Lord Lothian was at Segaon (Sevagram), he had asked to Mahadeva Bhai to give a copy of *Hind Swaraj*, for as he said, "all that Gandhiji was teaching now lay in the germ in that little book which deserved to *be read and re-read* in order to understand Gandhiji properly."[10] Gandhiji himself circulated the booklet among his English and Indian friends and published their comments and criticisms in the *Indian Opinion*.[11] After his return to India, Gandhiji continued to refer to *Hind Swaraj* in his personal discussions, public speeches, letters and prefaces he wrote from time to time. In 1914 when the second Gujarati edition was published, he wrote : "I find that the convictions as stated in the book have grown stronger."[12] In 1919 he was rather much convinced in 1919, that "what he had said about machinery in *Hind Swaraj*" is *literally* true."[13] Answering to his critics in 1920, he said : if the countrymen follow the methods adopted in *Hind Swaraj*, "they would have *Swaraj* not in a year but in a day."[14] In 1921, in his Foreward to the book, though he pleaded that he is "not aiming at destroying railways or hospitals, though I would certainly welcome their natural destruction. Neither railways nor hospitals are a test of a high and pure civilization. At best they are necessary evil. Neither aids one inch to the moral stature of a nation."[15] In 1922, reply to a leaflet on

Gandhi raj, Gandhi tried to reconcile between his ultimate ideas and the practical. *Hind Swaraj* is a manifesto of an alternative civilization. Railways, hospitals and machinery are the symbols and trade-marks of the modern civilization. Hence Gandhi's wrath against them can be understood in the holistic perspective. "It is not right therefore to tear some ideas expressed in the Indian Home Rule from their proper setting, caricature them and put them before the people as if I was preaching these ideas for anybody's acceptance."[16] Though he vehemently criticized the institution of doctors and modern medical institution, he did not hesitate to seek their advice in time of need" but it does not mean that he has completely agreement with his views expressed earlier. He says : "I have nothing to withdraw from what I have written in the Indian Home Rule."[18] The Indian Home Rule depicts the ideal state but so long we do not come up to the ideal condition, we have to compromise with imperfections like modern state, modern democracy, modern medicine and modern educational system. But he was convinced that : there is not one word in Hind Swaraj that cannot be substantiated. If I have to rewrite it today (1920), I may change the language but never the thought."[19] (letter to Satis Chandra Dasgupta). In 1938, the *Aryan Path* did a distinct service by bringing out a Special Number on *Hind Swaraj* by inviting foreign authors to express their views on it. There were trenchant criticisms as well as the highest appreciation but Gandhi remained firm. He said : I may change the language here and there, if I had to rewrite the booklet. But after the stormy thirty years through which I have passed, I have seen nothing to alter the views expounded thereon."[20]

The contributors to the *Aryan Path* special Number were eminent thinkers as Frederik Soddy, the well-known Chemist and Economist; G.D.H. Cole, the eminent English author and thinker, C. Delisle Burns, John Middleton Murry, J.D. Brestford, Hugh Fausset, Claude Houghton, Gerald Heard, and Irene Rathbone.[21] On the whole, the book appealed to all these European authors who even expressed their doubts on many of Gandhi's formulations. In 1939, when a friend charged Gandhi of contradiction between what he wrote and what he practiced, Gandhi explained that though his ideal is "to see beauty in voluntary simplicity, poverty and slowness," he shall never reach it myself and hence cannot expect the nation to do so." Being a highly practical man, he did not avoid railway travelling or motoring for mere sacking of looking foolishly inconsistent.[23] In 1948, he wrote to Krishna Chandra, he explained it more clearly : "I still abide by whatever I wrote about railways, etc. in *Hind Swaraj*. But that applies to the ideal state. This possible that we may never reach that state. Let us not worry about it.

If we do not have railways and other facilities, we should not feel unhappy. We must use these facilities as little as possible. There will be all types of people in our society... we have to live with them."[24] The last letter he wrote to Jawahar Lal Nehru in which he referred to *Hind Swaraj* on October 5, 1945[25] to which Nehru's reply dated 9th October 1945 shows that Nehru could not appreciate the seriousness contained in the Hind Swaraj or he had his own views.[26] On November 13, 1945, Gandhi again wrote to Nehru from Poona after some discussion.[27] After Gandhi's death, *Gandhi Marg*, the Journal published by Gandhi Peace Foundation, organized a symposium and *three* broad and rather well-articulated trends emerged.[28] The participants were eminent Indian thinkers like Badurddin Tayabji, R.C. Majumdar, D.R. Manekar, R.K. Patil, Kodanda Rao, R.R. Diwakar, Sugatdas Gupta etc. The editor was Mr. T.K. Mahadevan. In April 1982, Gandhian Institute of Studies, an organization founded by Jaya Prakash Narain and supported by Sarva Seva Sangh, organized a three day Seminar on April 20-22, 1982 at Rajghat, Varanasi in which, Devadutta, Ramashraya Roy, P. V. Pillai, J.P.S. Oberoi, K. Raghvendra Rao, Indira Rothermunal, Mira Sinha, Ramjee Singh, Hitesh Ranjan Sanyal, T.K. Oommrn, Y.D. Snsnyhu, R.K. Paul, Kishan Patnayak, Buddhadeva Bhattacharya, B.P. Pandiya, Kishan Saint, Sunil Sahasrabuddhi and the last but not least, Nageshwar Prasad, the Director of the L.I.S. contributed.

Fortunately the papers and discussion has been published in book form—*Hind Swaraj a Freshlook,* by the Gandhi Peace Foundation ably edited by Dr. Nageshwar Prasad with a learned long Introduction.[29] Again, *Indian Society of Gandhian Studies,* an all India body of Gandhian Intellectuals and academicians, during its annual conference held at Gandhigram Rural Institute from 9th to 11th January 1988, had chosen *Hind Swaraj* as the main theme for the Conference.

Gandhi Jyoti, a Journal of the Department of Gandhian Thought, Bhagalpur University, Bhagalpur brought out a Special Number on *Hind Swaraj* incorporating some of the important papers submitted to the said Conference held at Gandhigram.[30] In 1997, Anthony Parel has brought out an outstanding publication on *Hind Swaraj and other writings* containing Editor's Introduction (XIII-LXII), a Note on the history of the Text (LXII-LXII), Principal Events in the life of M.K. Gandhi, Biographical Synopsis, and text of *Hind Swaraj* with editor's notes, (14-125) and Supplementary writings (129-193). It has been published as Cambridge Text in modern politics.[31] It is by far the most authentic script of the *Hind Swaraj* with necessary information and editorial comments, only equal to Dr. Nageshwar Prasad's *Hind Swaraj : A Fresh Look.* Of late, there has been a spurt in organizing discussion through symposium or seminar on the concept of *Swarajya* from historical[32] and philosophical standpoints,[33] with learned participants like Prof. Daya Krishna, D.P. Chattopadhyaya, Kiret Joshi, Ravindra Kumar, C.P. Bhambri, Mohini Mullick, Rajendra Prasad, Ramayan Ghosh, Ramjee Singh, S.R. Bhatt, Shashi Prabha Kumar, Harbans Mukhia, P. C. Joshi, Bhuvan Chandel and others. Perhaps there has been a national trend to understand the concept of *Swarajya* and along with it Gandhi's *Hind Swaraj.* Dr. Makrand Paranjape of I.I.T., Delhi has also published a book on *How to read 'Hind Swaraj.'* It contains twenty chapters.[34] According to the author, reading is not an innocent affair, it is a serious engagement which involves some crucial choices. Reading *Hind Swaraj* literally, accepting every word of it as gospel would result in great inner turmoil. On the occasion of 125th birth day celebration at Bhopal in M.P., there had been a programme on Hind Swaraj and a small booklet has also been published entitled—*Fir se Hind Swaraja*[35] (Hindi) or *Hind Swaraj, Again*. There have been some more smaller publications here and there on *Hind Swaraj* like *Hind Swaraj Ka Jan Path*.[36]

As Gandhiji's private secretary Sri Mahadeva Desai in his *Preface* to the new edition of *Hind Swaraj* has acknowledged that the *Special Hind Swaraj Number* of the *Aryan Path* is "unique in its conception and beautifully successful in its execution."[37] It owes its appearance to the devoted labours of Srimati Sophia Wadia who sent copies of *Hind Swaraj* to numerous friends abroad and invited their views on the book. The result is remarkable and the Special Number has become truly special as it contains articles by some great thinkers and well-known pacifists and socialists. The articles are so arranged "that adverse criticisms and objectives raised in earlier articles are mostly answers in subsequent ones."[38] But there are one or two criticisms which have been made practically by all the writers. Briefly, to Professor Soddy the whole approach was some kind *utopian vision*, yet at the end of his survey, he felt that "any one who wishes to change the world would do well to study it."[39] G.D.H. Cole did not subscribe to the view that "western civilization is of necessity at enemity with human soul"[40] and yet he admitted that "Gandhi's case against the west looks infinitely stronger than it looked to us."[41] He' therefore felt that the book had "a deep power to disturb—much deeper than it could have had when it was written."[42] Delisleurns, reacting to Gandhi's unwarranted condemnation of machinery, said "This is a fundamental philosophical error. It implies that we are to regard as morally evil any instrument which may be misused... Any mechanism may be misused, but if it is, the moral evil is in the man who misuse it, not in the mechanism."[43] However, he advised the west that it would be a very great advantage in English and American politics as well as conduct of industry and common life in the west if the influence of such a man as Gandhi were to spread among us.[44] John Middleton Murry pointed out certain contradictions in Gandhi's approach to non-violence, machines and his acceptance of village community as a form of self-rule. He also raised a deeper question saying that "the efficacy of non-violence quickly exhausts when used as a mere technique of political pressure." However, he acclaimed the book as "one of spiritual classics of the world,"[45] and "the greatest that has been written in modern times."[46] J.D. Bradford very much doubted if "as a matter of practical service to the present condition of India, Gandhi's gospel preached by Gautama to India"[47] Hugh Fausset' while doubting the approach to machinery appreciated that *Hind Swaraj* aims at restoration of man to his true state and regarded *Hind Swaraj* as "one of the best modern handbook of the real revolution which must happen in us all, if we are to fulfil the creative purpose of life."[48] Claude Houghton welcomed the underlying message of Hind Swaraj *i.e.*, love, and generally approved of the doctrine of passive resistance.[49] Gerald Heard discovered in Gandhi's ideas then beginning of a new world-order and described *Hind Swaraj* as superior to Rossean's *Social Contract* and Karl Marx's *Das Capital*.[50] Irene Rathbone acclaimed the book as "enormously powerful and by its 'tremendous honesty' forced her" to search her own honesty. Of late Dennis Dalton regarded it as a proclamation of ideological independence."[52] and Judith Brown certified "the nearest he came to producing sustained work of political theory"[53] and Catlin went to compare it to the Spiritual Exercises of St. Ignatius Loyala[54] Chapter IV of *St. Mathew* or *St. Luke*.[55]

In the *Gandhi Marg* symposium on *Hind Swaraj*, three broad trends emerged. First was an attack on the 'development model' of the west viewed "from the standpoint of total resources available to mankind :[56] and development in the western sense was as "an illusory and unrealizable one.[57] As against this trend, some participants termed Gandhi's prescription as simply impracticals and his attitude was illogical, unreasonable and unhistorical which had vitiated all his conclusions and recommendations.[58] Finally there were those who were willing to incorporate some of the policies but were opposed to implant them in toto.[59]

It will be interesting to note down the chronology of the publication of the text of *Hind Swaraj* in various languages. It is as follows :

1909—Hind *Swarajya*, Gujarati, 13-22 Nov. 1909 on board *Kildonan Castle* Published in two installments in the Gujarati section of *Indian Opinion*, 11 and 19 December, 1909.

1910—Published in book form on 20 January, 1010—International Printing Press, Phoenix, Natal, Gujarati text banned on 24.3.1910 English trans. By Gandhi under the title *Indian Home Rule* with Preface + Forward, Phoenix Natal, 20.3.1910. On the title page of the English translation, Gandhi changed the Gujarati title from *Hind Swaraj* to *Hind Swaraj*, perhaps to come nearer to the popular speech.

1914—Second Gujarati Ed. With a new Preface, Phoenix Natal.

1919—First Indian edition of *Indian Home Rule* with a new *Forward* by Gandhi and a Note by C. Rajgopalachari, published by Ganesh & Co. Madras by dropping 1909 *Foreward* and 1910 *Preface.*

1921—First Hindi Translation of Hind Swaraj with Preface and Note. Navajivan Press, Ahmedabad. In a Young India editorial of 26th January and gave the English text the new title Hind Swaraj or Indian Home Rule Nalesan & Co. and Tagore and Co. (both Madras) brought reprints of 1919 Indian edition.

1924—An American edition under the title of *Sermon on the Mount* ed. Haridas T. Mazumdar with an Introduction by Hohn Haynes Holmes published from Universal Publishing Co., Chicago.

1938—Revised New Ed. With a Preface by Mahadeva

Desai 11.12.1930. The ban on *Hind Swaraj* was lifted on 21.12.1938. (MSS No. 65 Nehru Museum, Delhi).

1939-Navajivan Press, Ahmedabad, reissued the Revised New Edition, *The Collected Works of Mahatma Gandhi*, Vol. X, 1963; Oxford ed. Of *The Moral and Political Writings of Mahatma Gandhi*, by Raghvan Iyer, 1986.[59]

Context

For a proper understanding of *Hind Swaraj*, it is necessary to be acquainted with the historical context in all its dimensions—political, social and international.

On the *international plane*, behind the Russo-Japnese war,[60] there was the obvert signs of the revolutionary fervour in Czarist Russia which finally led to the Bolshevik revolution. Perhaps, communism was the first ideologically organized challenge against the Euro-American imperialism and capitalism in the world. In a way it was a people's liberation movement on the international level. We have seen its fruition in 1916 Russian revolution. However, we have also to consider the impact of the Double Revolution—The French Revolution and the Industrial Revolution besides the Intellectual Ferment in the rise of socialism—Babeuf (1960-97), Phillipe Bounarott (1761-1836), Saint Simon (1760-1825), Fourier (1772-1837), Robert Owen (1771-1850), Proudhan (1809-1865), Wilhelm Weetling (1808-71), Auguste Blanqri (1805-1884), the Chartist Movement in Great Britain (1836-53), Adam Smith and David Ricardo, Hegel, Young Hegelians, Feurbach etc.[61] However the most important feature is publication of the *Communist Manifesto* (German ed. 1872, 1883, French 1848, English 1888, American 1871) etc. Whatever the historical antecedents of the Manifesto may have been, it is more important to study it in the light of its influence on the world during the span of over 150 years. The Second Congress of the Communist League (London, Nov.-Dec. 1847) gave Marx the task of drawing up the new "Confession of Faith" as the official programme of the League. Before, this effort of the *League of the Just* (Paris, 1838), *Communist*

Correspondence Committee (Brussels, 1846) and the *Communist League* (June, 1847) and the publication of Engels' *Principles of Communist* also have to be taken into consideration. The *Manifesto* is divided into four chapters. The first chapter having 54 paragraphs reviews the rise of the bourgeoisie on the ruins of the feudal system of the property relations, government and morality which if destroyed, shows how 'the powerful and colossal productive forces' which the bourgeoisie itself created have now grown to a point where they are no longer compatible with bourgeoisie property relations. The *Second* chapter of the *Manifesto* contains 76 paragraphs proclaims the policy of the Communist Party. The *Third* chapter surveys and takes issue with other recent existing schools of socialist thought, the reactionaries, the Utopians and the humbugs. The *Fourth* chapter is a brief postscript of the relations of Communists to other radical democratic movements.[62]

Hence the *Communist Manifesto* and the *Hind Swaraj* as the *Gandhian Manifesto* have to be studied side by side along with their background, the influences of their respective philosophical traditions, the influence of thinkers and impact of their cultures etc. Before, we begin to discuss the ideological context of Marxism, that there is a great degree of agreement between their anti-elitist, non-exploitative, anti-imperialist and pro-poor attitudes. Not only England but most of the western countries like France, Germany, Spain, and Holland etc. were imperialistic and capitalist powers. Liberation from the yokes of imperialism and capitalism was the greatest challenge before Marx and Gandhi.

Hence, the ideological background of *Hind Swaraj* is very important for its proper understanding. It comprehends both Eastern and Western, ancient and modern sources and it has a wide canvas from religion (Hinduism, Jainism, Buddhism, Christianity, Islam, etc.) and theology, dialectics to dietetics, critique of industrial civilization to civil disobedience, Basic Education and art criticism etc. He was intensely a religious soul but he was never sectarian or even an evangelist missionary. Whatever might be the Indian values in the past, the mind of India was deeply stirred by several new developments in the West[63]—both technological and cultural. For instance, the railways, hospitals, law courts, industrialization, modern educational system, parliamentary systems of governance and the western style of life had overpowering influence over the Indian mind. There was a great urge to imitate the west and transform India on their model. However, side by side, a national renaissance had swept across India which was the result of national resurgence. Raja Ram Mohan Roy, Ishwar Chandra Vidyasagar, Swami Dayanand (Arya Samaj), Swami Vivekanand (Ramkrishna Mission). The Theosophical Movement, etc. contributed a lot to remind the Indian people of their great spiritual and cultural heritage. Gandhi tasted the rival pulls of two civilizations representing two world-views and two ethos and values. Modern civilization forms the broad historical context of *Hind Swaraj*.[64] It is a critique of western civilization and is regarded as the main contributions to modern political thought. No doubt the tone of his criticism is harsh and even intemperate and is likely to mislead the reader. No doubt Gandhi has his own definition of civilization "that mode of conduct which points out to man the path of duty (*Sudharo*)[65] Barbarism (*Kudharo*) is the absence of civilization. "Performance of duty and observance of morality are convertible terms. To observe morality is to attain mastery over our mind and our passions.[66] Here Gandhi very much eulogises the value of ancient Indian civilization. He puts in nutshell his experience: "A man is not necessarily happy because he is rich or unhappy because he is poor." The rich are often seen to be unhappy, The poor to be happy."[67] Here he lands the teachings of ancient Indian moral and spiritual seers who always dissuaded us from luxuries and pleasures. Here extols the values of ancient Indian civilization beyond measure. He goes to say that nothing can equal the seeds sown by our ancestors. Rome went, Greece shared the same fate; the might of the Pharaolis was broken; Japan has become westernized; of China nothing can be said; but India is still, somehow on other, sound at the foundation."[68] Alas! Gandhi would have changed his statement of self-righteousness about India of today. Today, India is more materialist than the west. True to his apprehensions, that his "first complaint is that India is becoming irreligious... we are turning away from God."[69] Speaking about the present condition of India, Gandhi said : "It is a sad condition. In thinking of it my eyes water and my throat gets perched. It is my deliberate opinion that India is being ground down, not under the English heel, but under that of modern civilization."[70] Gandhi had perhaps much more concern for civilizational torpor or decay than anything else because he knew that imitating western materialism and consumerism will be detrimental to India. In 1908, he wrote that western civilization is only a hundred years old, or to be more precise, fifty,"[71] and it has developed innumerable cracks and contradictions. *First*, instead of having a holistic concept of *Nature-animals-Man* relationship, which has sustained our evolutionary scheme so far, we are speaking in terms of "conquest of Nature", with the result that we have tragic scenario of *Nature Vs Man* or vice-versa. This has created unprecedented environmental problems as well as a dangerous psychology towards limitless consumerism. Economic prosperity has come to be regarded as the sole criterion of human progress while our ancient seers had opined us about the virtue of *voluntary limitation of wonts*. Gandhi's dictum "Nature has enough to meet our needs but not our greed" has therefore been the most cherished slogan of every environmentalist today. The object of politics today is to achieve maximum material prosperity for the satisfaction of our desires. In order to achieve this object, the so-called civilized nation of the western world justified 'imperialism and colonialism,' while adopting 'liberalism and democracy' for their own countries. They invented many mischievous theories like *Pax Britannica* or *'while man's burden'* and 'superiority of—western morality, political economy, and other western civilizational values, on the basis of which they got a self-ordained right to rule over India.[72]

Hence, the task of Gandhi was to strike at the very root of this 'modern civilization' so that it branches like colonialism, consumerism, and wrong notions about 'development' and 'progress' might fall off themselves and save the Indians from imitation. Gandhi says : "If India copies England, it is my conviction that she will be ruined."[73] He further warned : "we want English rule without the English men. You want tiger's nature, but not the tiger, that is to say, you would make India English."[74] Hence the encounter between India and Britain is posited in terms of an encounter between two civilizations."[75] Gandhi tried to argue that India's culture is a culture of restraint and peace; it disfavoured urban living and opted for rural living, preferred *soul-force* rather than *brute-force*. Here kings and their swords were inferior for sword of ethics and used soul-force as a political weapon by the people of India.

Although Gandhi had basic foundation of Indian ethos and civilization, however the most crucial formidable period of his ideas were digested and crystallized in South Africa, where had both first hand experience of the working of western civilization, as well as his studies of the works of the western critics of the industrial life and consumerism. While Indian thought influenced his metaphysical and ethical visions, his socio-economic thinking were greatly influenced by Tolstoy, Ruskin, Thoreau, and Edward Carpenter etc.

Gandhi's views are more akin to those of Tolstoy than to those of Ruskin and others.[76] Rev. J.J. Duke calls Gandhiji a disciple of Tolstoy[77] and Gandhiji himself considers an "elevated admirer who owes much in life to him.[78] Gandhi himself admits : Next to the late Raychandra, Tolstoy is one of the three moderns who have exerted the greatest spiritual influence on my life."[79] Gandhiji read Tolstoy's *The Kingdom of God is Within You,* when he believed in violence and was passing through a crisis of scepticism but its reading cured him of his scepticism and made him a firm believer in Ahimsa.[80] Both Tolstoy and Gandhi denounce modern civilization as based on force and exploitation; both are opposed to violent methods of fighting evil; both lay stress on the reform of the individual purity of means, simplicity, bread labour and virtual celibacy. Tolstoy's philosophy of Christian anarchism, is the application of the teachings of the Sermon on the Mount—the core of which is "Love". This is similar to *Ahimsa* of Gandhiji. Gandhi was in correspondence with Tolstoy. According to Tolstoy, the only way to make the world happy is to bring about a condition of the world wherein all beings could love others more than they love themselves."[81] Like an anarchist, Tolstoy condemns the state and its machinery, law courts, police and military, private property and capitalism, even the schools, as well as all these offend against the law of love. He is against the use of force, payment of taxes and compulsory military service, organised society. Here we can see Gandhi's condemnation of the symbols of modern civilized society like state.[82] Machinery,[83] Lawyer,[84] Modern education,[85] Brute Force[86] etc. in the Hind Swaraj. Tolstoy even goes further and is against legitimate marriage which he calls "domestic prostitution." In *Kreutzer Sonata,* Tolstoy denounces sexual love as the worst sins and pleads that the relation between man and wife should be transformed into brotherly and sisterly affection. Tolstoy's *The Kingdom of God Within You* deeply impressed Gandhiji and cured his scepticism. Therefore, Gandhi treats Tolstoy as "the greatest apostle of non-violence that the present age has written or spoken on non-violence so fully or so insistently and with such penetration and insight as he. I would even go further and say that his remarkable development of this doctrine puts to shame the votaries of *Ahimsa* in this land of ours.[87] *"The Kingdom of God is Within You"* was made mandatory for the members of the Phoenix Settlement and later Gandhi had it translated into Gujarati.[88] Three other works of Tolstoy listed in the Appendix of Hind Swaraj—*How shall we Escape? The Slavery of our Times,* and the *First Step* and his *letter to a Hindoo* are essentially criticism of various aspects of the new industrial civilization-dealing with the evils of exploitation of workers, the degradation of the peasants, the absence of virtue of moderation, and rampant consumerism.[89]

Tolstoy's commitment to non-violence is extra-ordinary uncompromising. Tolstoy thinks that "it is not English who have enslaved the Indians, but the Indians have enslaved themselves",[90] because the Indians "recognized and still recognize, force as the fundamental principle of social order" as they submitted to their little *rajahs,* and on their behalf struggled against one another, fought the Europeans and the English. Here Tolstoy was critical of Indian revivalism which to him had injected some narrow sectarianism and to some amount of martial tendencies. Gandhi shares this idea in *Hind Swaraj* under Chapter VII *Why was India Lost?*

Next to Tolstoy, Gandhi got the determining influence to change his life in accordance with the ideals of John Ruskin's book *Unto This Las* (1860). He translated it into Gujarati entitling it *Sarvodaya.* Two of books has been written Ruskin—*A Joy For Ever and its Price in the Market* (1857) published under the title *The Political Economy of Art.* The work markes the beginning of Ruskin's Critique of the industrial civilization he pleaded for providing for the basic needs for food, shelter and clothing, pleasant object, of minimum luxury, healthful rest, and serviceable leisure in that order. He was critical that the modern political economy as a science of labour management provides for luxury of the few and it does not seem capable to satisfying the basic needs of the many. This also inspired Gandhiji in adopting the doctrine of appropriate technology and cottage and village industries. However, Ruskin's *Unto This Last*[91] had a "magic spell" which he read in 1904 on a night journey from Johannesburg to Durban and deduced the three principles (1) The good of the individual is contained in the good of all. (2) That a lawyer's work has the same value as the barber's (3) That a life of labour is the life worth living. Gandhi not only read the book as an intellectual recreation. He rose with the dawn, ready to reduce these principles into practice."[92] This he did similar after completing his seminal book *Hind Swaraj.* He wrote with commitment : "My conscience testifies that my life henceforth is dedicated to its (Swaraj) fulfillment."[93] Hence

Gandhi's paraphrase of Unto This Last should be understood as a prelude to *Hind Swaraj*. Gandhi resembles Ruskin in several aspects *(a)* Both preach supremacy of the spirit and trust in the nobleness of human nature, *(b)* both emphasis the priority of social regeneration to mere political reform, *(c)* both greatly distrust machinery, *(d)* both insist that the capitalist should adopt a wise paternal attitude in relation to his employees[94] *(e)* both had their priority as the Last Man.

Gandhi read extensively both in South Africa and England about "the new industrial civilization" as well as his own cultural inheritance of Indian civilization in spite of the warning of Tolstoy contained in the controversial "Letter to "Hindoo" to be cautions about cheap revivalism, Gandhi read Henry Sumner Maine's classic *Village Communities in the East and West*, Dadabhai Naoroji's *Poverty and the Un-British Rule in India* and *Economic History of India* by R.C. Dutt.[95] Gandhi used Maine's thesis, firstly to unemphise that *Swaraj* would mean little for India if the lives of the poor in the villages saw no significant improvement.[96] Secondly, he found support for his argument that Indians in South Africa are the inheritors of a civilization that had prosperity as well as representative democracy.[97] Besides, Gandhi read Edward Carpenter, Max Nordan, Godfrey Blount, Thomas Taylor and Robert Harborough Sherard (all listed in the Appendix of *Hind Swaraj*). Edward Carpenter's *Civilization : Its Cause and Cure*[98] viewed civilization as a *'disease'*. However, Gandhi retains the metaphor but modifies its use—modern civilization is a *curable disease*.[99]

Blount's pamphlet *A New Crucade* advocated 'simplicity', art, aspiration." Its motto—"the betterment of society begins with the betterment of the individual," country life is the best term of the good life", "handicrafts and agriculture are conducive to human well-being," machinery is the devil's instrument" and "Politics can only sent, never, initiate, social reform", "work is a form of liturgy while work without art is brutality[100] Thomas Taylor's *Fallacy of the Speed* (1909) challenges the prevailing assumption that *"faster is better"* like railway, aeroplane, shift of population from rural areas to new ugly urban slums. Taylor questions *'the fast life'*—"whether it is beneficial to live on a, high-speed basis' regardless of whether the result in their sum total are beneficial." Taylor asks, "Does quick locomotion finally tend more to give leisure or to destroy it?"[101] Similarly, Max Nordan being the author of *Paradoxes of Civilization*[102] is included in the Appendix of *Hind Swaraj*. In fact, it is an error for Nordan did not write any book under the above title. He wrote *"Conventional Lies of Civilization* in 1895 and *Paradoxes* in 1906. Gandhi might have read both *Conventional Lies of Civilization* is relevant here. Nordan exposes pessimism ingrained in 19th century. European civilization found in art, literature, religion, and politics.[103] The reason is a dichotomy between our thought and action, and the lack of truth in our lives. Modern civilization is more particular about form—dress, drawing room, furniture and wall-pictures, while the earlier civilizations was interested in manual work, simplicity, straight-dealing. "Today the cities grow at the expense of the farming population, and the attitude of the moderns towards manual labour is reprehensive."[104] Max Nordan charges the modern liberal professions, especially those of modern lawyers[105] and doctor,[106] of being parasitic.[107] This type of pessimism is also found in *White Slaves of England* (Being a True Picture of certain social conditions in the kingdom of England in the year 1897) written by Robert Harborough Sherard (1861-1943), which gives a harrowing account of the life of the average industrial worker in England, who share a common horrible slavery, the landlord's tyranny, poor wages and poorer health care. The condition of women was unimaginable appalling.[108] The title of this book is included in the Appendix in *Hind Swaraj* and there are ample references of about the contexts of this book in the 6th chapter of the *Hind Swaraj*.

Hind Swaraj has its American sources as well like Benjamin Tucker, the American anarchist and David Thoreau. Though Tucker is not mentioned in the Appendix of *Hind*

Swaraj, Tucker like Thoreau is a strong advocate of passive resistance for the oppressed masses for the reason that the modern governments with the power of bestowed upon men through service and technology can easily crush violent revolts but they cannot overcome passive resistance by military force. He also advocates non-payment of taxes as a method of civil disobedience and passive resistance. He is in favour of voluntary associations to restraint the unwieldy power of the State. Gandhi had read Thoreau's *Civil Disobedience* in South African prison from 10th Oct. to 13th Dec. 1908. He was the first to use the term *'Civil Disobedience'* in one of his speeches in 1949 advocating to refuge to pay taxes as a protest against slavery in America. However, Gandhiji had derived the idea of 'Civil Disobedience' (*Satyagraha*) before or independently and in order Gandhi used Thoreau's phrase—'Passive Resistance' to explain it to the English readers. But Thoreau's idea of Civil Disobedience revealed to Gandhi the possibility of using non-violence as a technique for solving even the major problems of social and political life.[109] Therefore, Gandhiji heard an echo of his own thought in Thoreau.[110]

Besides, Thoreau's mention in the *Appendix* of *Hind Swaraj,* he mentions Ralph Waldo Emerson in the *Preface.* Gandhi read Emerson's *Essays* very carefully in 1909 in the Pretoria Jail. He described Emerson's essays as the teaching of Indian wisdom in western garb.[112] Another author William Macintyre Salter is worth mention whose *Ethical Religion,* Gandhiji had paraphrased and published in an eight part series in 1907 in *Indian Opinion.* Many authors mentioned or discussed in his book included John D. Rockefeller, Jermy Bantham, Wendel Phillips, David Webster, Mathew Arnold, Emerson, St. Francis Xavier, St. Theresa, and Charles Darwin but Thoreau remained a lifelong. His principles of *Civil Disobedience* was paraphrased and published in 1907 in *Indian Opinion.* He was heartened to read that *conscience* not *majorities* should have the ultimate say in judging what is right and wrong, one's duty not go give support to evil or an unjust political regime, and the prison is the right place for the just person. Thoreau's another book *Life Without Principle* (listed in the Appendix) also impressed Gandhi. Thoreau believed that politics without virtue is "a kind of vegetation," and that "good manner cannot be a substitute for civic virtue. What mode, politics lacks is a 'high and earnest purpose' and an appreciation for culture more than for pafatoes."[113]

It would be injustice to overlook the influences of two great prophets of humanity, Socrates and Jesus upon Hind Swaraj. *Socrates was* a "great Satyagrahi, who practiced Satyagraha against his own people. His dedication to truth was unparalleled, so much so he became a martyr for truth. Gandhi wrote a small booklet on *Satyaveer Sukarat* (Socrates—the Hero of Truth). Similarly, Gandhi was tremendously influenced by Jesus and his Crucification. Jesus fought with love *i.e.* non-violence, we can say that Gandhi was Socrates and Jesus Christ of modern times. Gandhi also saw no difference between the Sermon on the Mount and the Gita..." Today, supposing I was deprived of the Gita and forgot all its contexts but had a copy of the Sermon, I should derive the same joy from it as I do from the Gita". To him 'Christianity's particular contribution is that to achieve love. No other religion says so firmly that God is love and the New Testament is full of the word."[114] Gandhiji calls Jesus the Prince of Satyagraha and said that he would not hesitate to call himself a Christian if he had to face only the Sermon on the Mount and his own interpretation of it."[115] (London, 1930, p. 93) Christianity's particular contribution is that of active love. No Other religion says so firmly that God is love and the New Testament is full of the world.[116] The entire teaching of the Christ logically follows from his conception of the universal, loving fatherhood of God and the brotherhood of man. If we remember the two commandments—"Thou shalt love thy God", and "Thou shalt love thy neighbour as thyself, we come to the central basis of non-violence. Jesus' prayer at the alter of Crucification : "Father, forgive them, for they know not what they do."[117]

Gandhi's interest in Christianity was deep both in thought and action. He not only under took a serious study but was greatly appreciative of their effort to make religion socially practical. He admires Joseph Doke's disinterested social service, he himself learnt the art of nursing as a compounder from Lanalot Booth, an Anglican priest for the whole year two hours daily. His contact with Catholic monks and nuns of Mariannhill was so inspiring that when he was back in India he would hold out Marianhill as a model for institution devoted to Harijan service.[118] Needless to say, he did not approve high pressure evangelism of the missionaries.

Gandhi's acquaintance with Hellenic thought was perhaps limited to Plato's *Apology* listed in the Appendix of *Hind Swaraj*. He found in it the "qualities of an elixir", [119] who paraphrase was published in *Indian Opinion* in six parts in 1908 and later as a pamphlet under the title "Story of a Soldier of Truth. So far its influence on *Hind Swaraj* is concerned, it is philosophical that there is moral link between the *order in the soul* and *order in society*, and the doctrine of ultimacy of inner conscience and the option to suffer harm rather than to inflict it.[120] Gandhi was deeply influenced by the martyrdom of Socrates. His small book *Satyabir Sukrat* (Socrates, the hero of truth) is inspiring. Socrates was perhaps the first martyr of truth. Socrates, no doubt is an exemplary *Satyagrahi*. Similarly Gandhi seems to be Socrates reborn.

Gandhi had also same links with the peace-loving *Quaker Community*, to whom pacifism and non-resistance are basic principle. They also believed that each man's life is guided by an inner light.[121] Quaker's experiment in administering the state of Pennsylvania was a source of strength in focusing the concept of a non-violent state. Similarly, Gandhi also came into contact with the *Theosophists*, for their attempt to find out the "essential unity of all religions." There were other groups and persons, who were either to runners of Gandhian philosophy or contemporaries. For example, the French revolutionary Anselem Bellegaregne (Mid 19th Century) anticipated Gandhi's political technique. He believed that all government was based on violence and hence was an evil and preached the "theory of calm" to overcome the govt. by the refusal of assistance, *i.e.* by abstenation and inertia."[122] There is no birth of pacifist thinkers even in the modern times like Aldoux Huxley, Charles Maine, Roland Host, Meijer Wietman, Gerald. Heard etc. but pacifism in the west suffered a setback when during the world war, such great personalities and otherwise peace-lovers like Bertrand Russell, C.E.M. Joad, Roman Rolland went to support military collaboration of well-armed states, while Gandhi consistently tried to appeal to "Hitler"[123] or to "Every Japnese"[124] to desist from such killings. He had most denounced the use of Atom bomb.[125] Gandhi had discovered the moral equivalent of war" but he had yet to perfect the science of "civilian defence" to meet the foreign invasion.

The Indian Roots of the Hind Swaraj

No doubt Gandhiji gathered ideas from all over the world but his thought were deeply rooted in Indian ethos and culture. The very word *'Swaraj'* which finds place in the title of the book is a Vedic word which means 'self-rule'. Gandhi says : Swaraja is when we learn to rule ourselves. Real 'Home Rule is self-control'[126] is a sacred word meaning self-rule and self-restraint and not freedom from all restrains which independence often means. He further says "Govt. over self is the truest swaraj; it is synonymous with *Moksha* or salvation.[127] It means purification, self-restraint or govt. ourself. It no doubt means 'rule of the people' but it also means 'the rule of justice.[128] Hence the first slip to *Swaraj* lies in the individual[129]. Hence Gandhi's *Swaraj* has strong moral and spiritual dimensions. It has also cultural context. Hence in cultural mythology, *Ram-rajya* is described as the ideal of *Swaraj*. During the period of modern Indian Renaissance, Swami Dayanand, Swami Vivekananda and many oriental thinkers thought and wrote upon the theme of *Swaraj*. Hence during the freedom struggle, *Swaraj* became the most popular national slogan. Dadabhai Naoroji, the Grand old Man of India, had voiced the demand of 'Swaraj' as early as in 1906 and during the great national agitation against vivisection of Bengal Province by Lord Cürzon. 'Swarajya' became the war-cry of Indian Independence struggle.

It owes, the Gandhi's definition of *Swarajya* as the "rule of the mind over itself and its passions" is derived from the Gita—the characteristics of the 'steadfast wisdom'[130] which is the picture of the ideal person who strives to attain inner *swaraj.* Gita's distinction of self (*Atman*) from the body (*deha*) is the basis of differentiation of Brute-Force vs Soul-Force in the *Hind Swaraj.* (Ch. XVI). Next to the Gita, *Sri Ram Charita Manas* of medieval Indian poet and saint Tulsidas had the strongest influence in his religio-ethical development. One of the first books published by his International Press, Phoenix, Natal was an abridged version of Tulsi's work, He wrote : "We wish that every Indian goes devoutly through the summary which we are placing before the public, reflect over it, and assimilate the ethical principles so vividly set out in it."[131] No doubt Gandhi derived the basic tenets of Indian philosophy and culture through the studies of the *Upanishads.* Patanjali's *Yoga-Sutra, Manu-Smrti, Yoga-Vasistha* and specially of the Chapter on *Panchikaran, Mani Ratna Mala, Mokshamala* (on the advice of Roychandraji) he looked to the Gita and the Ramayana as the constant source of guidance. In fact, what is the Gita description of *Sthitapraina* (steadfast wisdom) in an abstract manner, it is beautifully but concretely depicted in the personality of Ram. This style of governance is ideal (*Ram-rajya*) or *Swarajya.* Gandhi had began reading texts of Indian philosophy in London through English translation like *the Song Celestial* and the *Light of Asia* both translated by Sir Edwin Arnold, the *Life of Mohamet and His Successors* by Washington Irving, Thomas Carlyle's life of the Prophet in Heroes and Hero-worship and the Heroic History and *The Saying of Zarathusta* (Boston). Born in a traditional Hindu Vaishnava family, Gandhiji was influenced by Hindu ethics and metaphysics. Though he was catholic enough to admire the basic teachings of all religions, according to him, "Hinduism satisfies my soul, and fills my whole being and I find a solace in the *Bhagawadgita* and the Upanisadas that I miss even in the Sermon on the Mount... When doubts haunt me, when disappointment stare me in the face, and when I see not one ray of light on the horizon, I turn to the Bhagvadgita, and I find a verse to comfort me, and I immediately begin to smile in the midst of overwhelming sorrow."[132] Of all the books that have moulded in life, the Gita comes the first, with which his first acquaintance was in England in 1888-89 through English translation by Edwin Arnold. Later on he studied and endeavoured to live up to its teachings till his life. He regarded it as his "spiritual reference book."[133] However, it is unique that Gandhiji derived, out of an epic of war like the Mahabharata and the Gita because to him, the theme of the Gita is self-realisation through action without desire for the result *Anasakti* or *Niskama-Karma*. He came to the conclusion that "it is not possible to kill your brother after having killed all your passions[134]... The result of this selfless detachment must be uttermost truth and non-violence."[135] Perhaps, to Gandhi, non-attachment and non-violence go together.

The Gita message of *Karmayoga* and *non-violence* is rooted in the teachings of the *Isa-Upanisad*, which can be regarded as its metaphysical basis. The Upanisada in general and *Isa-Upanisad* in particular believe in the doctrine of spiritual immanence and Universal Soul and the conviction that "all life is one." If we have a vision of such universality or oneness, there is absolutely no scope for hatred or anguish with anybody.[136] Hence non-violence follows as the sine qua non from the concept of Universal Soul which finds its genesis in the Rig Veda and its famous Purusa-Sukta. Hence Ahimsa—ethics has a strong metaphysical basis in the Hindu thought. Whether it is the Upanisada, or the *Yoga*-Sutras of Patanjali or the epics of the *Ramayana* and the *Mahabharata, Ahimsa* finds a place of pride in the cardinal virtues. To Gandhiji *Isa-Upanisad* was the most vital source of thought as it provided not only the metaphysical basis for non-violence but also a robust defence for the Gita's ethics of *Anasakta-Karma-Yoga.*

Isa Upanisad unambiguously says that we cannot shun action so long we have our physical bodies; hence what is necessary is to practice our duty without attachment. This is the quintessence of Gita also. Gandhiji studied the yoga aphorisms in 1903 at Johannesburg. He found that *"Ahimsa"* is included in the five *Yamas,* but Gandhi's ingenuity lies in developing them into *Eleven Disciplines* for the Satyagrahis, called Eleven Vows (*Ekadasa Vrata*). Besides the Five Principal Disciplines (*Yama*). Gandhiji has added six others—"Control of Palate" (*Asvada*) which is perhaps helpful to observe and maintain the vow of celibacy (*Brhmacharya*). But adding 'fearlessness' (*abhaya*) shows Gandhi's great spiritual insight and his manliness. A man commits wrongs when he is under fear of loosing property or power, or even life. Hence the Vedas exhort us to be fearless—*Ma-bhaih* (do not fear). Even the Gita teaches us to be fearless. Krishna exhorts Arjuna not to be downcast and give up weakness of the heart. Another important vow of *dignity of labour (Sarira-Srama)* is added which has both a personal as well as social significance. We have already discussed the spiritual-ethical and social significance of dignity of labour which are ingrained in Indian thought and culture. Gandhiji has inherited it and given new dimension and social significance. Apart from these ethical principles, Gandhiji has introduced three social virtues which were and still are the most relevant today like the practice of untouchability *(asprsya-bhavana), treating all religions with equal respects* (Sarva-dharma-samabhava) and giving priority in using things made of one's neighbourhood (*Swadeshi*). Taken together these eleven ethical principles form the basic fabric of Gandhian philosophy of life. Whether it is the traditional Hindu faith or the Jainas or the Buddhist believe in these moral ideals. The Jainas prescribe the Five-fold Great Vows (*Mahavratas*) and many smaller vows (*Anuvratas*), so also the Buddhists believe in the Five-fold Principles (*Panch-shila*) and Ten Principles (*Dasa-shila*). They are similar to the five cardinal virtues which we find in the Upanisads, Yoga-Sutras, the Epics etc.

In the modern times, Gandhiji had Gopal Krishna Gokhale as his political guide (Raj Guru) and spiritual companion as Rajachandra. They have, no doubt provided the spiritual ground for *Hind Swaraj i.e.,* the faith in the 'soul-force', 'spiritualisation of politics' and a defence of religious way of life but they could not influence the structure of Hind Swaraj. It was mostly his own. Gokhale did not like it and said that Gandhi will himself revise it when he reads it again. There were many other eye brows raised from other Indian leaders and scholars.

Gandhiji established some social-spiritual centres called *Ashramas* for a formation of new Gandhian personality and community. They are the laboratories for preparing committed and dedicated comrades for 'non-violent resistance' as well as non-violent 'social reconstruction'. These Ashramas were almost self-reliant based on dignity of labour and community life. Without anybody's personal possessions, there was two such settlements in South Africa—(1) *Phoenix Settlement* (1904) outside Durban city, where *Hind Swaraj* was first in developing a sense of all-India consciousness without regionalism and the worst manifestations of caste mentality a legacy of Indian social systems. It was here that Indian women were able to find liberation from a number of social taboos. To quote Gandhiji himself : "Phoenix is intended to be a nursery for producing the right men (and women's and right Indians Phoenix is a more suitable place for making experiment and gaining proper training." (C.W. 9.382). There was no untouchability, no high and low. We all know that the even orthodox people had to forget customary restrictions in matters of food and drink with Muslims, Christians and the untouchables. Here in the Ashram, the "all India mind" with a secular and radical outlook was being prepared. (See Prabhudas Gandhi's book *My Childhood with Gandhi,* Ahmedabad, 1957.

(2) *The Tolstoy Farm* was established in 1910 outside Johannesburg in South Africa on land donated by his friend Kallenbach.

(3) *The Sabarmati Ashram,* was established in January 1915 at the outskirt of Ahmedabad and closed down permanently when Gandhiji set out for Dandi March to break Salt Law. It exists as the reminiscent monument.

(4) *The Sevagram Ashram* near Wardha (Maharastra) was founded in 1936.

He was so much impressed with Ruskin's book that he serialized a nine-parts paraphrase in *Indian Opinion* and later published it as a pamphlet under the title *Sarvodaya* first in Gujarati, then in Hindi etc. He gave its title for the sake of Indians who did not know English. Literally Sarvodaya means 'universal welfare', which also depicts the ideal of Indian culture—*Vasudhaiva Kutumbakam,* the whole world is the family.

Modern Indian Renaissance and the Hind Swaraj

Modern Indian Renaissance is basically a robust quest after a common Indian identity. We can, to an extent, call it a sort of just and needed revivalism. Gandhi's *Hind Swaraj,* apparently is also in the same line but its originality and beauty lies in "reconstruction" rather than blind following or adoration of the past. Here he is more a *rebel* than an status-quoist of all traditional Indian values and social customs. For example, Dr. R.C. Majumdar was critical of Gandhi's stand on modern civilization and the Hindu-Muslim problem. Gokhale himself was upset about his crude critique of western liberal democracy and civilization. We are also aware of the debate between Gandhi and Nehru on the social policy suitable for a free India. The entire band of religious extremists, both Muslims and Hindus did not see an eye to eye with him while Gandhi stood for a composite Indian culture and a united composite India. Gandhi was from the very beginning opposed to *two nation theory in his own way,* while the Muslim League advocated that "Hindus and Muslims were two nations" so did the Hindu communalists calling themselves 'nationalists' also believed that Hindus and Muslims are two nations and therefore they strongly adovacated for the establishment of a *Hindu-Rastra*. (Hindu State) they had no qualms for non-violence also. They were drawn more towards adopting 'revolutionary violence' as a method of achieving independence, perhaps being disenchanted with the method of 'prayers and petitions' adopted by the Indian National Congress. This is also evidenced by the split in the Congress between the Moderates and the Extremists in 1907. The Moderates defined *Swaraj* within the Empire -called 'dominion status' and that through 'constitutional means'. Their important leaders were A.O. Hume, Sir William Wedderburn, Dadabhai Naoroji, Gopal Krishna Gokhale, Badruddin Tayabji and others, while the Extremists were led by B.G. Tilak, Sri Aurobindo Ghose and others. They stood for 'complete independence' outside British Empire and they had no hesitation in advocating 'other means' than constitutional methods. Besides they also became advocates of Indian revivalism. Tilak revived Ganapati festival in the memory of Shivaji, the last fighter of the Hindu-Kingdom called *Hindu-Pad-Padsahi*. Sri Aurobindo was himself a revolutionary who edited *Vandematram*, appealed to *power (Shakti)* in its creative but violent forms. Besides, there were a number of expariate Indians, who were surcharged with patriotic zeal and fervour. They were influenced by European revolutionary movements and ideas like terrorism, Marxism, ideologies of the Irish 'home rule' and the Italian *'Risorgimento*. Then there were many brilliant youths though who had had gone abroad for their careers, were drawn towards the revolutionary movement because of their nationalist fervour. At home, they became active supporters of revolutionary organizations like *Abhinav Bharat Anusilan, Yugantar* etc. They were engaged in all sorts of revolutionary activities. Among they were Shyamji Krishna Varma (1857-1930), V.D. Savarkar (1883-1966), Madan Lal Dhingra (1887-1909), Madame Bhikaji.Camma (1861-1936), V. Chattopadhyaya (1880-1937), Tarak Nath Das (1884-1958) etc. Shyamji while in England, apart from organizing revolutionary work, instituted 5 Herbert Spencer Indian Fellowhips each valued Rs. 2000/- each, and 6 other Fellowships valued Rs. 1000/-. The object of these endowments was to bring bright Indian youths for training in the methods of violent revolution. Varmaji also founder of India House (1905) in London to offer residential facilities for these youngmen. He also founded a revolutionary monthly called *The Indian Social* in 1905 dedicated to propagate Spencer's ideas as absolutely essential for modernizing India with the two masterhead quotations of Herbert Spencer. One was like a war-cry : "Resistance to aggression is not simply justifiable but imperative Non-resistance hurts both altruism and egoism."[137] Though initially Gandhi and Varma were friendly, till 1906, it deteriorated beyond repair by 1909, so much so that a leading article in Varma's *Indian Sociologist* (Oct. 1913) denounced Gandhi's philosophy of non-violence as being utterly subversive of all ethical, political and social ideals." The brain behind this revolutionary group was V.D. Savarkar who went to London in 1906 as recipient of Shivaji Scholarship on B.G. Tilak's recommendations. He lived at India House till his arrest and deported in 1910. He wrote two books : one a translation of *Mazzini's Life* from English into Marathi only two months before Gandhi's arrival in London in May 1909. A militaristic interpretation of *The Indian War of Independence of 1857* was his another book. Madan Lal Dhingra (1887-1909) an engineering student from prestigious Imperial College, London, being influenced by Savarkar and after being turned revolutionary assassinated the then Secretary of State for India on 1.7.1909. Only a few days before Gandhi's arrival in London. Gandhi openly denouncing this, wrote in the *Indian Opinion* "I must say that those who believe and argue that such murders may do good for India are *ignorant* men indeed. No act of treachery can even profit a nation. Even should the British leave the consequence of such murderous acts, who will rule in their place?" The only answer is : murderers. Who will then be happy? Is the English bad because he is an Englishman? Is it that everyone with a Indian skin is good? If that is so we claim no rights in South Africa, nor should there be any angry protest against oppression by Indian princess. India can gain nothing from the rule of murderers—no matter where they were black or white."[138]

In the *Hind Swaraj* also Gandhi has reiterated "those who believe that India has gained by Dhingra's act or other acts in India make a serious mistake. Dhingra was a patriot, but his love was blind. He gave his body in a wrong way; its ultimate result can only be mischievous."[139] He further emphasized : "Many people exalt at the explosion of bombs." This only shows ignorance and lack of understanding. If all the British were to be killed, those who will kill them would become the masters of India, and as a result India would continue in a State of Slavery. The bombs with which the British will have been killed will fall on India after the British."[140] Gandhi has devoted the whole of XVI chapter as the critique of "Brute Force" in *Hind Swaraj*. One of the high points of the entire work is that Gandhi rejects the modern principle of reason of state or "national interest" as a legitimate principle of international politics."[141] Secondly, his response in denouncing the application of brute force even for a good cause for achieving national freedom is based on his article of faith that there is an unavoidable connection between *ends* and *means* as opposed to the hedonistic doctrine that end justifies the means. Gandhi wrote to Polak in clear terms : "Mr. Dhingra's defence (by the Indian revolutionaries) was inadmissible. He was egged on to do this act by ill-digested reading of worthless writings. It is those who incited him to this that deserve to be punished." (C.W. 9302) Sri Aurobindo's fiery articles in *Vandematram* in Calcutta is well-known. He attended in 1907 Stuggart International Congress of Sociologist and moved a resolution for Complete Independence for India which was seconded by Comrade A.M. Hyndman, a British Marxist leader. Madame Bhikaji Rustom Cama was a pioneer women leader in Indian politics and she came from a smallest majority Parsi Community. Mr. C. Chattopadhyaya, who was brother of Sarojini Naidu, called the nightangle of India for her sweet and sonorous voice, edited another monthly called *Talwar* (Sword). Unfortunately he met his triage death at the hands of Soviet firing squad. There were other revolutionaries abroad working for India's freedom. At home, we know that there was a powerful trend of Indian revolutionaries like

Sardar Bhagat Singh, Rajguru, Sukhdeo, Asfaqullah. Chandra Shekhar Azad, Khudi Ram Bose, Ram Prasad Bismil, Sachindra Nath Sanyal, Yatindra Nath and many others all over the country.[142] In 1942, after the leaders were arrested, the people got uncontrolled and at many places arson, violence were let loose. However, when Gandhi was preparing to write the *Hind Swaraj*, he had to face the revolutionary for more than one reasons. Firstly, he thought that method of violence is *unspiritual, unethical* and *anti man*, and it is also counter-productive in practice. He was also convinced that Indian nationalism is never anti-British or anti-western. Truth is neither the monopoly of the East nor of the west. So he took all the ingredients of the East and the West and tried to weave them into a coherent philosophy, which was free from narrow nationalism on the one hand, terroristic violence and modern materialism on the other. Gandhi was fully supported by Tolstoy in his commitment to non-violence for achieving India's freedom. Tolstoy was also convinced that non-violence is the only legitimate means available to the morally upright conscience. The great Indian terrorist Tarak Nath Das (1884-1958) of *Anusilan* group together with V. Chattopadhyaya refuted Tolstoy's thesis in *Vande Matram*. In fact Tolstoy had written his famous controversial *Letter to a Hindoo* (1908) in response to a letter from *Das* as editor of his journal *Free Hindustan*. Tolstoy did not approve either the method of violence or sticking to sort of revivalism" in the name of nationalism. Gandhi was as much a *nationalist* as an *international*. He was a reformer but not revolutionist. He loves Indian culture as basically Indian culture is strongly rooted in spiritualism. He was critical of western civilization as it was based on materialism and brute-force. No doubt, he welcomes many of contributions like the development of science, stress on civil liberty, equality, rights, economic welfare, liberation of women from tradition and religious tolerance, but he would like to harmonise rights with duties, reason with intuition, science with spirituality, freedom of religion with equal respect for all religions and so on. He was very much enamoured by two things nursing and constitutional government and the rule of law, which he found in the British colonialism but he did not accept the materialistic and hedonistic life-style, and over stress upon rights and reliance on brute physical force. Hence, he would never accept either the theory of *Pax Britannica* or superiority of western culture. He would not accept that only the 'industrialized' world is 'civilized'. However the Industrial Revolution affected not only 'the mode of production' but also the 'mode of life'. Perhaps technology and ideology go together. Hence Industrial Revolution ushered an 'epistemological revolution' which in turn paved the way for political, religious and social revolutions also. But the root philosophy of industrial revolution was the notion of "conquest of nature" for its maximum exploitation for maximum satisfaction of human needs, comforts and luxuries. The Indian Renaissance as understood by Gandhiji, has a different world-view and a different style of life. It is neither narrow sectarian nationalism nor some sort of *Pax Indica*. Similarly, the religious world-view of Indian Renaissance is universalistic. Swami Ramkrishna and Swami Vivekananda advocated the cause of "Universal Religion", so also Tagore talked of the "Religion of Man." The Indian Renaissance do not like to work like political Christianity or Political Islam which even tried "to displace all other religions that came in their way either through warfare", or organised evangelical work. True there is a list of Christian critics of Christianity like Thomas Moore, Voltaire, even Jefferson but the theories of Jihad, conversions and iconoclasm is still pervading some fundamentalists Islamic organizations like Taliban in Afghanistan or extremists in Bosnia, Chechnia etc. Of course, the Sufi-cult in Islam is very catholic and there are many Muslim countries where secular ethos prevail but the world has to go a long way towards religious reconciliation. The Indian Renaissance wants to assert its national and cultural identity which is neither fundamentalist nor unaccomodative and does not prefer violence to solve this problem. Conversion or reconversion called *Shudhi* is perhaps unknown to the Hindu ethos and it is a form of reaction and distortion. But there are religions like Buddhism, Islam and Christianity who openly believe in conversion should try to reconsider their positions.

"The Christian missionaries justified conversion not merely by referring to the "fundamental rights of man" but by citing the many factors of superiority of their religion. This is different from the India views-point. Any way, we can conclude that "although conversion is not intrinsically wrong if it happens as a result of genuinely religious inspiration, but it is extremely difficult to decide the Tightness of it in most cases. So conversions wrought through organizational propaganda and institutional approaches may have undesirable consequences, besides being non-religious in their motives and methods."[144]

Dharmapal in his recent book *Despoliation and Defaming of India : Legacy of Nineteeth Century British Crusade*, has shown with supporting documents from three Britishers in India like William Wilberforce (1813), James Mill (1817), and Thomas Babimngton Macaulay (1833-1893) that their main aim was to conquer the minds of Indians, their language, and culture and to make them feel inferior in comparison to Western Society."[145] In his famous essay *Foundations of the Govt. of India, 1883*, also wrote in similar vein said : "The introduction of such a civilization into India, the *Pax Britannica*, has the great and characteristic task of Britain in India.[146] All these were challenges to Gandhi to speak for culture of India. He is a little hyperbolic (to my mind) but when challenge comes, one has to speak in a different tone. Speaking about the merits of Indian civilization, he says : The civilization India has evolved is not to be beaten in the world."...He further says "It is a charge against India that her people are uncivilized, ignorant and stolised, that it is not possible to adopt any changes. It is a charge really against our merit."[147] He says : "India is still, somehow or other sound at the foundation, because its subscribes" to the concept that *artha* and *kama* (wealth and desires) should be based on *Dharma*.[148] (Righteousness)

The Purpose of Writing Hind Swaraj

Gandhi was a man of action. So whatever be thought or wrote was a guide to action. He did not believe in intellectual gymnastic or writing for writing's sake. He had neither time nor any inclination for indulging in Utopian thinking or scholastic thinking. He wrote *Hind Swaraj* because he could not do without it. So it was written at one stretch with a furious speed so that when the right hand got tired, he continued with the left, 40 of the 275 manuscript papers were written by the left hand.

So he wrote as if under *inspiration*. John Middleton Murry speaks about Gandhi's "profound experience of illumination" and compare it to Rosseau's *On the Road to Vincennes*.[149] Gandhi himself felt that he had produced "an original work"[150] writing to his friend Henry Polak a month before the actual writing Gandhi wrote—"I, therefore, feel that I should no longer withhold from you what I call progressive step I have taken mentally... After all they are not new but they have only now assumed such a concrete form and *taken a violent possession of me*." In the Foreward he says : "I have written because *I could not restrain myself*.. Just as one cannot help speaking out when one's heart is full, so also I had been unable to restrain myself from writing the book since my hearts was full."[151] It was because of this that Middleton Mury acclaimed the book as one of the "spiritual classics of the world" and the "greatest that has been written in modern times," like the *Spiritual Exercises* of St. Ignatius Loyola, and Chapter IV of St. Mathew or St. Luke.[152] However, this was his subjective consideration in writing the book.

His objective aim in writing this book is to clarify the meaning of Swaraj. The concept of 'Swaraj' has been coming down since the time of the Rig Veda and some Upanisads. Even during modern Indian Renaissance, the concept of *Swaraj* appeared again and again. Gandhi's *Hind Swaraj* is the "rule of the people, is the rule of justice."[153] Hence "Swaraj" is a sacred word meaning self-rule and self-restraint and not freedom from all restraint which independence often means."[154] To Gandhi, it is synonymous with *Moksha* or salvation. Govt. over self is the truest *swaraj*.[155] Swaraj has many facets—economic, political, social and moral, which Gandhi calls the *Square of Swaraj*. To him, mere withdrawal of the English is not independence. It means the consciousness in the average villager that he is the maker of his destiny, he has his own legislator through his clusen representatives.[156] Mere by political independence he does not mean either imitation of the 'British House of Commons', far less the then 'Soviet rule of Russia' or the Facist rule of Italy, or the Nazi rule of Germany. He has described it as *Ramraj i.e.*, sovereignty of the people based on pure moral authority.[157] His ideal of political governance described in the name of *Swaraj* means the government by the consent of people ascertained by the largest numbers of the adult population, male or female, native born or domiciled, who have contributed by manual labour to the service of the state and who have taken the trouble of having their names registered as voters.[158] Swaraj government will be a sorry affair if people look up in it for the regulation of every detail of life.[159] His Swarajist frame is not formal, it is "poor man's *Swaraj*"[160] or economic democracy. So also it is social democracy which recognizes no race or religious distinction. Nor is it to be the monopoly of the literate persons nor yet of manual men. *Swaraj* is to be for all, including the farmer, but emphatically including the maimed, the blind, the starving, toiling millions.[161] However, his *Swaraj* is not narrow and aggressive nationalism. "Purna Swaraj is not isolated independence but healthy and dignified interdependence."[162] He was never in favour of India assuming the role of an imperialist power like England or France. His nationalism fierce though it was, it was neither exclusive, nor designed to harm any nation or individual. "Through *Swaraj*, we would serve the whole world"[163]—he said. He went further : "I would like to see India free and strong so that she may offer herself as a willing and pure sacrifice for the betterment of the world."[164]

Another very important and most immediate but negative impulse to write this revolutionary book is to present a counter manifesto of 'political terrorism' adopted by Indians at home and abroad. To Gandhi, adoption of violence is a 'suicidal policy.' In fact, *Hind Swaraj* originated in Gandhi's encounter with the Indian anarchists in England during his visit to London in 1909 to advocate the cause of South African Indians and mobilize British public opinion. At that very time, London was rocked by the murder of Sir Curzon Wyllis only nine days before. Madan Lal Dhingra, the assain had said that this was the only way left for achieving India's freedom. At the end of his statement he said, "I die, glorifying in my martyrdom."[165] Though the terrorist trace it to Indian heritage—the message of the Gita and the Ramayana to fight out injustice as part of practicing righteousness (*dharma*), but immediately they were dazzled by the heroic and nationalistic actions of Garibaldi and Mazzini in Italy. Shyamji Krishna Varma and Savarkar were the brains behind propagation of terroristic violence as the only effective method of achieving freedom. They were naturally disappointed by the Congress approach of 'political mendicancy' contained in the eternal programme of "prayer and petition". Gandhi found time to enter into a serious dialogue with this 'terrorist group' and tried to impress upon them the futility of their approach. Gandhi is on record to confess that : "I wrote the entire *Hind Swaraj*, for my dear friend Dr. Pranjivan Mehta. All the arguments in the book are reproduced almost as it took place with him."[166] In his message to *Aryan Path*, in which the *Hind Swaraj* was serialized, Gandhi says, "Let the reader bear in mind that it (*Hind Swaraj*) is a faithful record of conversations I had with workers, one of whom was an avowed anarchist. (Dr. Pranjivan Mehta)[167] Gandhi was also advised by Tolstoy to follow the path of non-violence in his *Letter to a Hindoo*, where he had adopted a practical commitment to non-violence. In chapters XIV, XV and XVI of the *Hind Swaraj*. Gandhi rejects the doctrine of violence both on ideological as well as on pragmatic basis.

In the background of this negative purpose of answering to the "Indian School of Violence", Gandhi had a positive purpose to expose the dangers of modern civilization because these youngmen were dazzled with the success of Japan which had achieved so much of progress by imitating the west, besides other western nations. In fact, the salvation for India, according to them lay in following the western path—western technology, western institutions like Parliaments, development models, and economics of scale; only the foreign dominion must end and the method to end it was through acts of terrorism. However, to Gandhi 'modern civilization with all the technology and institutions was far more dangerous than British colonialism. In fact, colonialism is a product of modern civilization. In fact, the key to understand *Hind Swaraj* lies in the idea that 'happiness' is different from 'pleasure'. Our real 'progress' does not consist only in acquisition of material comforts and luxuries. There is no limit to it. The more we get, the more we hanker after. It also leads to cut throat competition, social conflicts and wars. The U.S.A. for example with 6% of world population consumes between 30 and 50 per cent of world's annual production.[168] This is bound to lead inequality and exploitation. Over-consumerism leads to over-exploitation of natural resources leading to depletion of non-renewable resources and environmental pollution. This is highlighted by the publication of the Club of Rome thesis—*The Limits to Growth*. What Gandhi advocates in *Hind Swaraj* is supported and re-enforced by the *"Blueprint for Survival"*, [169] a statement by thirty three of Britain's most distinguished scientists. Hence G.D.H. Cole was obliged to say that "Gandhi's case against the west looks infinitely stronger than it looked to us, Westerners thirty years ago. The ideal of progress is related to the 'development model'. Hence Gandhi presents a contours of the *"whole theory of life"* which is in conformity with a spiritual "world-view". But this is not an attempt to go back to the so-called ignorant, dark ages. But it is an attempt to see beauty in voluntary simplicity, voluntary poverty and slowness."[171] This was Gandhi's ideal, which is opposed to the ideal of multiplication of wants, saving of labour with a view to having more and more leisure and large organization.

Another reason to write this book is to provide an "indigenous philosophy of independence". Hence, the title is typically in vernacular Indian language and the content is also indigenous. Instead of the Anglacised word "*India,* he has used the word—*'Hind'* and instead of the English word *"Independence"* or *"Freedom"*. Gandhi uses the term *Swaraj*—which has a long legacy from the time of the Vedas. It means that Gandhi wanted to usher an epoch of Indian Renaissance in its universal and spiritual perspective. He was never negative. He was never anti-British or anti-western. Like an incarnation, he came with a new message not only for India but for the whole world. For him *Swaraj* means the rule of righteousness or *dharma* free from superstition dogmatism and sectarianism on the one hand and ritualism and irrationalism on the other. As the Gita is a "book of duty" (*Karma-yoga*), so is *Hind Swaraj* a book of duties and obligation. Similarly, there is imprint of the Ramayana and its trans-humanism, piety and nonviolence on *Hind Swaraj*. Credit goes to Gandhi to interpret both these epics of war into the gospel of selfless action and love. In fact, "it is not a mere political book". He says himself "I have used the language of politics, but I have really tried to offer a glimpse of *dharma* what is the meaning of *Hind Swaraj?* It means the rule of *dharma* or *Ramarajya*. Therefore, he says : we may read the *Gita* or *Ramayana* or *Hind Swaraj*."[173]

Yet another purpose of writing this book is to present the picture of "India of His Dreams" or India after independence to the common man. Hence he did not enter into sophisticated and subtle arguments and polished language. He is open and straight which is the language of the common man in India. True Hind Swaraj cannot be taken as the final blueprint of Gandhi's social and world-order, it has to be expanded.

It has reference to an ideal state. But in substance his views remained the same. It contains the basis and fundamental propositions and which Gandhi tried to build up his whole philosophy of life these basics remain unchanged and unmodified. He was willing to make compromises on details but the basics remained the same. The ideals of Hind Swaraj might be too distant or Utopian to westernized and educated class of Indians but this is the common man's ethos and ideals. The common man of India believes in the ethical way of living and also have faith in spiritual power. Hence, Gandhi did not hesitate to expound the basic theory of "soul-force", "righteousness" and "non-violence". If we keep in our mind the ideological and the historical background, we will find it delightful as Plato's dialogue and as refreshing as Jesus Gospels.

REFERENCES

1. Paul, Anthony J., *Hind Swaraj and other Writings,* Cambridge University Press, 1997, p. XIV.
2. Gandhi, Prabhudas, *My Childhood with Gandhi,* Ahmedabad, 1957, pp. 87-88.
3. Murry, Middleton, J., "The Challenge of Gandhi" in *'Mahatma Gandhi,* ed. S. Radhakrishnan, Bombay; Jaico Publishing House, 1957, 2nd Ed., p. 325
4. Nanda, B.R., *Mahatma Gandhi : A Biography,* Delhi : 1974, p. 66.
5. *The Collected works of Mahatma Gandhi,* New Delhi : Publication Division, Govt. of India, Vol. X, p. 245.
6. Chatterjee, H., *Gandhi's Religious Thought,* London : 1992, p. 89.
7. Erikson, Erik, *Gandhi's Truth,* New York, 1969, p. 216.
8. Desai, M, "Preface", in M.K. Gandhi, *Hind Swaraj,* Ahmedabad, 1962, p. 14.
9. Parel, A., *Ibid.,* p. XIII.
10. Preface by Mahadeva Desai, to *Hind Swaraj* on 2.2.38, p. 13.
11. *Indian Opinion,* 21.5.1910 (Mr. Wybergh, Member Legislative Assembly, Transval).
12. *Hind Swaraj,* CWMG, Vol. XII, p. 411.
13. *Letter to Maganlal Gandhi,* CWMG, Vol. XV, p. 346.
14. Tendulkar, D.G., *Mahatma,* Vol. 11, p. 17.

15. *Hind Swaraj,* C.W.M.G., Vol. IX, pp. 277-78.
16. *Ibid.,* C.W.M.G., Vol. 23, pp. 38-39.
17. "My Mission", *Hind Swaraj,* C.W.M.G., Vol. 23, pp. 38-39.
18. C.W.M.G., Vol. 24, p. 548.
19. C.W.M.G., Vol. 42, p. 125.
20. A Message to *the Aryan Path,* C.W.M.G., Vol. 67, pp. 169-70.
21. Prasad, N., *Hind Swaraj : A Fresh Look,* Delhi : Gandhi Peace Foundation, 1985, pp. 8-10.
22. C.W.M.G., Vol. 70, p. 242 (The unbridgeable Gulf).
23. *Ibid.,*
24. C.W.M.G., Vol. 80, p. 325 (Letter to Krishnachandra).
25. C.W.M.G., Vol. 81, p. 319.
26. Nehru, J., *A Bunch of Old Letters,* London, 1985.
27. *Ibid.,* pp. 511-512 also Parel, Anthony, *Ibid.,* Gandhi-Nehru Letters, pp. 149-156 (Supplementary Writings).
28. *Gandhi Marg,* (Journal), Delhi, Oct. 1973.
29. Prasad, N. (ed.), *Hind Swaraj : A Fresh Look,* Delhi : Gandhi Peace Foundation, 1985.
30. *Gandhi Jyoti,* Hind Swaraj Special Number, Year-5, Nos. 283, 1988.
31. Parel, A., *Ibid.*
32. A National Seminar on The Freedom Struggle and Value-Thinking, Allahabad Museum, Allahabad, 2-3rd December, 1998.
33. Seminar on *Rethinking Swarajya,* 24-25 January, 2000 under the auspices of Indian Council of Philosophical Research, Delhi.
34. Paranjape, Makarand, How to Read '*Hind Swaraj?* I.I.T., New Delhi.
35. *Fir Se Hind Swarajya,* 125th birth anniversary celebration of Mahatma Gandhi, Bhopal (M.P.).
36. Tewari, Kanak, *Hind Swaraj Ka Janpath,* Bhopal, 1947.
37. Desai, M., Preface to the New Revised ed. of *Hind Swaraj,* p. 5.
38. *Ibid.,* p. 6.
39. *The Aryan Path,* Sept. 1938, p. 438.

40. *Ibid.*, p. 430.
41. *Ibid.*, p. 429.
42. *Ibid.*
43. *Ibid.*, p. 436.
44. *Ibid.*, p. 435.
45. Prasad, N. (quoted), *Ibid.*, p. 9 (Introduction).
46. *Ibid.*
47. *The Aryan Path*, p. 344.
48. *Ibid.*, p. 446.
49. Prasad, N., *Ibid.*, p. 10 (Introduction)
50. *Ibid.*
51. *Ibid.*
52. Dalton, Dennis., *Mahatma Gandhi : Non-violent Power of Action*, New York, 1993, p. 16.
53. Brown, Judith, *Prisoner of Hope*, New Haven, 1989, p. 65.
54. Catlin, George, *The Path of Mahatma Gandhi*, Chicago, 1950, p. 215.
55. C.W.M.G., Vol. 10, p. VIII.
56. Sugata Das Gupta, *Gandhi Marg*, Oct. 1973, p. 262.
57. R.C. Majumdar, D.R. Manekar, R.K. Patel, and Kodanda Rao, *Gandhi Marg*, Oct. 1973.
58. Prasad, N., *Ibid.*, p. 12.
59. Parel, A., "A Note on the history of the Text", p. LXIII-LXIV. *Ibid.*
60. Devadutta, "Hind Swaraj : Context and Text" in *Hind Swaraj : A Fresh Look*, p. 30.
61. Bhattacharya, B., *"Two Manifesto : Communist Manifesto and Hind Swaraj"*, Seminar on *Hind Swaraj*. Gadhian Institute of Studies, 20-22 April, 1993, p. 2.
62. *Ibid.*
63. Prasad, N., *Hind Swaraj : A Fresh Look*, pp. 30-31.
64. Parel, A., *Ibid.*, p. XVII (Introduction).
65. *Hind Swaraj*, Ch. XIV.
66. *Ibid.*, p. 61.

67. *Ibid.*

68. *Ibid.*, p. 60.

69. *Ibid.*, p. 41.

70. *Ibid.*

71. *Ibid.*

72. "What representative govt. is a requirement of European civilization, while absolute government is that of Indian civilization."—The gist of Fitzgames Stephen's "Foundations of Govt. of India", quoted by Parel, A., *Ibid.* XIX (Introduction).

73. *Hind Swaraj*, p. 34.

74. *Ibid.*, pp. 28-30.

75. Prasad, N., *Hind Swaraj : A Fresh Look*, p. 34.

76. Dhawan, G.N., *The Political Philosophy of Mahatma Gandhi*, Ahmedabad : Navajivan, 3rd Rev. ed. 1957.

77. Doke, J.J., "Plodem Religious Pacifism, in *American Political Science Review*, June 1973, p. 3.

78. Gandhi, M.K., *Young India*, Vol. I, p. 652.

79. *Ibid.*, Vol. III, p. 843.

80. *Ibid.*, Vol. III, p. 830 (quoted by Mahadeva Desai).

81. Maudi, A., article on Gandhi and Tolstoy, in *Leader*, June 18, 1930, Refer Tolstoy's letter to Roman Rolland dated 4.10.1887 published in the *Modern Review*, January 1927.

82. Gandhi, M.K., *Hind Swaraj*, Ch. IV.

83. *Ibid.*, Ch. XIX, IX.

84. *Ibid.*, Ch. XI.

85. *Ibid.*, Ch. XVIII.

86. *Ibid.*, Ch. XVI.

87. Tendulkar, D.G., *Mahatma*, Vol. II, 2nd ed. 1961, p. 137.

88. Parel, A., *Ibid.*, p. Introduction XXXVII. He also got tanslated another book of Tolstoy—*What is Art?* Tolstoy's emphasis on experience and feeling, on the religious origin of art, on the need to communicate feeling through appropriate symbols, evoked in deep response in Gandhi's *Hind Swaraj*, Ch. XIV.

89. *Ibid.*, pp. XXXVIII-XXXIX (Introduction).

90. Tolstoy, *Letter to a Hindoo*, quoted by Parel, A., p. XXXIX.

91. This title came from *St. Mathew* 20.14.
92. Gandhi, M.K., C.W., Vol. 39, p. 239.
93. Gandhi, M.K., *Hind Swaraj,* Ch. XX 'Conclusion' last line, p. 104.
94. Dhawan, G.N., *Ibid.,* p. 31.
95. All listed in the Appendix of *Hind Swaraj.*
96. Mair, H.,Village Communities in the East and West, 1871.
97. Gandhi, M.K., *Complete Works of M. Gandhi,* Vol. I.93, 152, 164, Vol. III., 332, 341.
98. Originally a lecture delivered in 1889 to the Fabian Society.
99. Gandhi, M.K., *Hind Swaraj,* Ch. VI (Civilization), p. 38.
100. Blount, G., *A New Crusade,* 1903, Summarised in *Indian Opinion,* 1905.
101. Taylor, Thomas, *Fallacy of Speed,* 1909, p. 63 (See appendix) to *Hind Swaraj.*
102. Nordan, Max, *Conventional Lies of our Civilizations* (trans. From the Seventh German ed., London) 1895. This is the title, and not *Paradox of Civilization.*
103. *Ibid.,* p. 6.
104. *Ibid.,* p. 186.
105. See Ch. XI of *Hind Swaraj* on 'Lawyer's.
106. See Ch. XII of *Hind Swaraj* on 'Doctors'..."Its branches are represented by parasitical professions', p. 58.
107. Nordan, H., *Ibid.,* pp. 206-14.
108. Sherard, Robert H., *The White Slaves of England,* London, 1897.
109. Lal, B.K., *Contemporary Indian Philosophy,* Delhi : Motilal Banarsidas, 1973, p. 92.
110. Devadoss, T.S., *Sarvodava and the Problem of Political Sovereignty,* Madras : Univertiy of Madras, 1944, p. 74.
111. *Collected Works of Mahatma Gandhi,* IX. p. 240.
112. *Ibid.,* IX. P. 240.
113. Parel, A., *Ibid.,* Introduction, p. XLVI.
114. *Young India,* 31.12.1946.

115. Andreuej, C.F., *Mahatma Gandhi's Ideas,* London, 1930, p. 93.
116. *Young India,* 30.12.1931.
117. Luke, XXIII. 34.
118. C.V., 58, p. 261.
119. C.W., VIII.1.74.
120. Parel, A., *Ibid.,* XXXVI, Introduction.
121. Beals, C.A.C.F., *History of Peace,* London : 143, p. 31.
122. B.De Light, Conquest of Violence, London : 1938, pp. 100-110.
123. *Harijan,* 14.10.39.
124. Appeal to *Every Japanese, Harijan,* 26.7.42.
125. Gandhi National Museum, Delhi has brought out a leaflet quoting Gandhi at 28 places denouncing atom bomb in *What Mahatma Gandhi said about the Atom Bomb,* 1998.
126. *Young India,* 19.3.31.
127. *Young India,* 8.12.20.
128. *Young India,* 16.4.31.
129. Speeches and Writings of Gandhiji, Madras, Natesan, p. 409.
130. *Bhagwadgita,* II. 54-72.
131. C.W. IX. 98.
132. *Young India,* Vol. II, pp. 1078-79.
133. Desai, M., *The Gita According to Gandhi,* Ahmedabad, 1956, p. 122-23.
134. *Harijan,* 14.1.1939.
135. Barr, Murry, *Conversations and Correspondence with Mahatma Gandhi,* p. 14.
136. *Isa Upanisad,* Verse-7.
137. Spencer, H., *The Study of Sociology,* London, 1978, p. 168.
138. C.W. IX. 302-3.
139. *Hind Swaraj,* Ch. XV. p. 98.
140. C.W., Ch. VIII, p. 374.
141. Parel, A., *Ibid.,* Foot note Nos. 171, p. 87.
142. Gupta, Manmatrhnath, *Bharat Ke Krantikari,* Hind Pocket books, Delhi, 1984.

143. Lal, K.S. "Genesis of Religious Conflicts", *Dialogue,* New Delhi, Vol. II, No. 1. July-Sept. 2000, p. 92.
144. Pushparajan, A., *From Conversion to Fellowship,* Allahabad : St. Paul Publications, p. 298-299 (Epilogue).
145. Gangrade, K.D., Review of Dharmapal's book under title *Despoliation and Defaming of India : Legacy of Nineteenth Century,* Wardha Bharath Peetham, 1999, in Gandhi Marg, Vol. 21, No.3. Oct.-Dec. 1999, p. 376.
146. Parel, A., *Ibid.,* p. XX, Introduction.
147. Gandhi, M.K., *Hind Swaraj,* Ch. XIII, p. 60.
148. Parel, A., *Ibid.,* Pasilab Footnote No. 122.
149. Murry, John Middleton, "The Challenge of Gandhi", in *Mahatma Gandhi,* S. Radhakrishnan (ed.), London 1949, p. 429.
150. Gandhi, M.K., *Gandhi-Kallenback Correspondence* 1909-46, 4 Vols., New Delhi : Nehru Memorial Museum and Library, New Delhi.
151. C.W. 32, p. 489.
152. C.W., 10. VIII.
153. *Young India,* 164.31.
154. *Ibid.,* 19.3.31.
155. *Ibid.,* 8.12.30.
156. *Ibid.,* 13.2.30.
157. *Harijan,* 2.1.37.
158. Young India, 29.1.25.
159. *Ibid.,* 6.8.25.
160. *Ibid.,* 26.3.31.
161. Bose, N.K., *Selections from Gandhi,* Ahmedabad, Navajivan, 1957 (2nd ed.), p. 116.
162. *Young India,* 12.11.1931.
163. *Ibid.,* 16.4.31.
164. *Ibid.,* 17.9.25
165. Cited in James D. Hunt, *Gandhi in London,* New Delhi, 1978, p. 134.

166. *Speech at Gandhi Seva Sangh Meeting,* 21.2.1940, C.W. Vol. 71, p. 238.

167. *Prefce* to the 2nd ed. of *Hind Swaraj,* C.W. Vol. 67, pp. 169-70.

168. Sussane, Gowan, *Moving Towards a New Society,* Philadelphia, 1976, pp. 64-65.

169. Quoted a Sussane, Note 69, p. 89.

170. *The Aryan Path,* September, 1938, p. 438.

171. C.W. 70, p. 292.

172. C.W. 32, 489.

173. C.W. 32, 486.

5

Beyond Hind Swaraj

I

The last sentence of *Hind Swaraj*, differentiates this book from an arm-chair academics or utopia because Gandhi says : "my conscience testifies that my life henceforth in dedicated to its attainment."[1] This shows a sense of his commitment which necessarily implies a programme of action. No one realised better than Gandhi the tragedy of speculative thought without action and social action with personal commitment. Bulwer joins Gandhi when he says that "books are but waste paper unless we spend in action the wisdom we get from thought"[2]. That is why Gandhi and Gandhism without militancy is tantamount to reaction of the worst type and Gandhians without commitment are no doubt goody goody persons but merely happening status quo. Diwakarji is, therefore, right when he says that it is not only necessary *to experiment with truth* in our own life (satya sodhanam) but also *"to establish truth"* in society (*satya samsthapanam*).[3] Truth and non-violence were not only personal virtues but they have their societal character. Hence, non-violence without crusade against exploitation and corruption is lifeless pacifism. *Hind Swaraj*, reflects the real spirit of Gandhism because it is all war and no peace. It disturbs the status quo at every point and at every step. Hence the natural corollary of *Hind Swaraj* is struggle against injustice and exploitation against expansion of capitalism, economic and cultural imperialism, consumerism, militarian and the last but not the least *industrialism*, which is at the root of many of the vices stated above. Hence the task beyond *Hind Swaraj* was not of rewriting a second *Hind Swaraj* after studying the criticisms on this book but formulating and implementing action programmes or *Chhutakara*. Gandhi was approached from time no time to revise the book but he always confirmed the truth or what he wrote in 1909[4] and which he himself circulated in 1910 among his English and Indian friends. With his usual stubborn straightforwardness, he says : "I have nothing to withdraw from what I have written"[5] ..."there is not one word in *Hind Swaraj* that cannot be substantiated. If I have to rewrite it today, I may change the language but never the thought",[6] after the stormy thirty years through which I have passed. I have nothing to alter the views expounded therein"[7]... "I still abide by whatever I wrote about railways, etc..."[8] "My experience has confirmed the truth of what I wrote in 1909".[9]

II

These utterances of Gandhi reflect his sense of commitment hence professor Soddy's allegation that the approach in *Hind Swaraj* was some kind of utopian vision is unjust. Hind Swaraj is neither like Plato's *Republic* or Thomas Moore's *Utopia*, which are examples of very fertile imagination. To some extent, it can come along with *Communist Manifesto* whose primary purpose was not *contemplative enjoyment* of the existing world but its active transformation. These are critics who regard Gandhian prescriptions as simply impracticable because they think that various problems like unemployment, population growth, food shortage etc., could not be solved without resort to industrialisation. Some critics go so far to hold that all the evils we see in the type of development are usual and there was no need to reverse the process. However, recent critics of industrialisation have not only gone beoynd the evil effects of Urbanisation, Crime, social disorganisation, smoke and dirt, desolation of nature, exploitation of labour and others as were pointed out in the 19th century and in the beginning of the 20th century, they have reinforced many of Gandhi's apprehensions and objections who questioned the very basis of its dependence on the present-day technology. For example, the depletion of non-renewable resources has been highlighted by the publication by the club of Rome thesis *viz., The Limits of Growth.*

Many of the key mineral resources will be exhausted within the next 50 years. The world reserves of platinum, silver, gold, tin, zinc, lead, copper, tungsten, uranium 235, natural gas and crude oil will be exhausted by the end of this century.[10] The U.S.A consumes between 30 to 50% of world's annual production,[11] although it has only 6% of world's total population. This is supported by the "Blueprint for Survival", a statement by 33 top scientists of Britain. They warn that "continued exponential growth of consumption of materials and energy is impossible. Present reserves of all but a few metals will be exhausted within 50 years if consumption rates continue to grow as they are. Obviously, there will be discoveries and advances in mining technology, but these are likely to provide us with a limited stay of execution".[12] It means that industrial technology of large scale industries have been responsible for depleting natural resources. Through mechanisation of agriculture, there has been "Rape of the Earth" degrading the soil (Jacks & Whyte). The other most dangerous hazard of indusrialisation is environmental pollution. Our entire global eco-system has been seriously endangered. Apart from releasing tons of toxic materials from radio-active elements of hundreds of nuclear reactors, they have posed a threat to our very existence.

Thus nuclear power and nuclear weapons are inextricably linked. Fritjob Capra, therefore, holds industrial technology responsible for severe degradation of eco-system and impending global extinction due to continuing proliferation.[13] To think that if industrialisation is socialised, it would be free from the evils of capitalism, is wrong. Gandhi says : "The economic imperialism of single tiny island kingdom (England) is today keeping the world in chains. If an entire nation of 300 (now 780) millions took to similar economic exploitation, it would strip the world bare like locusts."[14] It means that according to Gandhi, exploitation was due not only because of capitalist mode of production but also because of the very nature of present day machine technology. Hence, socialisation or nationalisation was not a guarantee against exploitation. Besides, Gandhi also questioned the "values of increased productivity or "multiplication of needs", which has become the characteristic feature of modern civilization. But we must remember that "the mind is a restless bird; the more it gets the more it wants, and still remains unsatisfied. The more we indulge in our passions the more unbridled they become."[15] The Indian seers therefore, set a limit to our indulgences. In fact, happiness is largely a mental condition. "A man is not necessarily happy because he is rich, or unhappy because he is poor. The rich are often seem to be unhappy, the poor to the happy".[16] It is perhaps in the spirit that the Bible says—"Blessed are the poor...". It is not perpetuating poverty in society but freeing the whole society of the limitless consumerism and wants. Recently, SPAN magazines of U.S.A has reported that as many as 25 million people in U.S.A alone have opted for some sort of voluntary simplicity cutting down their retirements for their happiness. It reminds us of Socratis reply to a question as to "what is the secret of happiness?" and his reply was : "How many things you can do without?" Regarding Bertrand Russell's plea for minimising human labour trough maximising technological perfection to secure more time for time recreation as well as for cultivation of knowledge of science and culture, Gandhi had his reservations. He felt that "if we set our hearts after such things, we would become slaves and loose our moral fibre."[17] The Indian in the pst after due deliberation decided that we should only do what we could with our *hands* and *feet*. They saw that "our real *happiness* and *health* consisted in a proper use of our hands and feet". [18] They further reasoned that "large cities were a snare and a useless encumbrance and that people would not be happy in them."[19] Today it reminds us of Spengler's warning in his masterpiece *Decline of the West* that unwieldy cities are signs of a perishing culture. Gandhi calls them 'cages of human spirit and fountain of devitalization and delinguency. It is a pathological phenomena". Schumacher advocates that *Small is Beautiful*. John Galbraith while warning against the made rush for industrialisation says" : "Sabbath was made for man, not for Sabbath". This means that industry should not be made an end in itself. Hence according to Gandhi, "it behoves every lover of India to cling to the old Indian civilization even as a child clings to the mother's breast."[20] The ancient Roman and Greek civilisations perished because they had opted for materialistic and hedonistic ways of life while Indian civilization, despite the ravages brought by foreign domination has kept its head high, because, civilisational ideal of India lays stress upon duty and morality. Morality is not something transcendental, it is to attain mastery over our mind and our passions. Hence Gandhi's *Hind Swaraj* is a manifesto of freedom of India from moral and spiritual slavery. Gandhi's denunciation of railway, machinery, professional institutions such as lawyers, doctors should not be taken literally. They are unblematic and have metaphorical significance. Gandhiji has used rather crude language about machinery and we cannot therefore, say that "machinery" was a 'moral evil'. So replying to a question whether he was against all machinery, Gandhiji said : "How can I be when I know that even this body is a most delicate piece of machinery? The spinning wheel is a machine...What I object is the craze for machinery, not machinery as such."[21] "Machinery was welcome only if it did not lead to concentration of wealth in few hands."[22] We could invent, occupy and use science and technology...without exploitation....without loosing mastery over them.[23] He was "socialist enough to say that such factories should be nationalised, state controlled...The saving of the labour of the individual should be the object, and not human greed the motive."[24] His criterion for dividing line which machinery to accept or not was simple—"Just where they cease to help the individual and encroach upon individuality."[25] Taking into consideration this amount of flexibility in Gandhi's approach the machinery, we cannot brand his criticism against industrialisation either as subjectivistic or unreasonable. A recent Unesco study point out at the "lack of Community satisfaction" in modern industrial civilisation, where more than 60% boredom and 90% work without understanding immediate significance. Material advancement does not mean moral progress.

However, the theme of Hind Swaraj is not just the moral inadequacy and extravagant pretensions of modern civilisation, but its teacherously deceptive, hypnotic and self-destructive tendency. But to call this analysis simply as subjectivistic or moralistic is unjust. In fact, it is based on sociological and psychological findings. G.D.P. Cole, who did not agree with Gandhi that 'Western civilization is of necessity at enemity with human soul" admits that "Gandhi's case against the West looks infinitely stronger that it looked to us, Westerners thirty years ago."[26]

III

What to speak of the Utopias, even Communist Manifesto, which avowedly proclaims not only to interpret the world but also to change, it, lacks the amount of personal commitment and involvement as Gandhi did demonstrate throughout his life. No doubt, Marx exhorted the Proletariat to action but he himself assumed the role of a friend, philosopher and guide and could not involve him self into active struggle as Gandhi did. Marx will be remembered as a master theoretician, hence Vinoba calls him as the great seer *Maha Muni.* Gandhi derived all his theories from experience and practice. The Communist Manifesto, like any other book is addressed to others, especially to the workers. In the Hind Swaraj, the primary initiator and actor is Gandhi himself. In any Gandhian action, the initiator must be *"the Self of the person* engaging in this action."[27] Gandhi was engaged throughout his life in a bitter struggle and search for modes and principles for a more human life beyond modernity.

He exhorted as well as indulged into action programme as he felt that "strength will be available to him who will act".[28] He is not to be downhearted with the views of Western personalist philosophers like Martin Buber who believe that mankind has no choice in the matter of modern industrial civilization, "that a reality once created cannot be avoided and has to be lived through in relationship in order to reach the crest beyond."[29] He was prepared to continue his fight even alone. If there be only one man, he can fight because thought it as a Satanic civilisation. He believed that "Indian civilization is the best and that the European is a nine day's wonder. Such ephemeral civilizations have come and gone and will continue to do so. "[30] This is based not on the force of the soul but on brute.

For achieving *Swaraj*, Gandhi presented a 19-point programme of Action entitled *Chhutkara* in Gujarati, which means the "emancipation or liberation". He is convinced that there is no ground for Pessimism and despondency, because "only the fringe of the ocean has been polluted, it is those who are within the fringe alone need cleansing."[31] The vast majority of the farmers and village dwellers have not been polluted and they still adhere to the life-values of Indian culture. The "polluted minority" are the lawyers, doctors, the wealthy and the like which was affected by the Western civilizationbut even they were eager to have *Swaraj* and Gandhi enunciates 19 Point Programme of action for them as cleansing operation. The doctors, the lawyers, the bureaucrats, the technocrats, the rich, and the professional parliamentary politicians are the creatures of modern industrial civilizations who belong to the non-productive parasitical middle classes. They are the most trusted bodyguards of Western civilisation. But they constitute a minority. If they change their life-style, *Swaraj* can easily come to us. Hence, Gandhi programme of action concerns only his polluted minority. He classifies the entire programme of action under four heads.

***(a)* Liberation from foreign language** : The first and foremost item of liberation is liberation from the English language. Language is closely connected with life and our culture. We cannot communicate our ideas and emotions through the medium of a foreign language. "The foreign medium has caused brain fag, put an undue strain upon the nerves of our children, made them crammers and imitators unfitted than for original world and thought, and disabled them for filtrating their learning to the family of the masses".[32] Gandhi further says that "the foreign medium has made our children practically foreigners in their own land."[33] It has prevented the growth of our vernaculars. Unless we advances the cause of the vernaculars, "We shall not be able to remove the growing intellectual and cultural gulf between our men and women and between the classes and the masses. The vernacular medium alone can stimulate originality in thought in the largest number of persons."[34] Therefore, as the first and foremost item of liberation asks the 'polluted minority' to make use of the English language only on rarer occasions. [35] Needless to say that 95% of people do not know English and even those who know donot use in day-to-day discourse and work.

***(b)* Liberation from the lawyers** : Gandhi wants to free Indian people from the lawyers because, according to him, "that lawyers have enslaved India, have accentuated Hindu Mohammedan dissensions and have confirmed English authority"[36] They will, as a rule, advance quarrels instead of repressing them. They are glad when men have disputes. Petty pleaders actually manufacture them. Their routs like so many beaches, such the blood of the poor people. But the greatest injury they have done to the country is that they had tightened the English grip, [37] because it would not have been possible for the English to carry on their Government without law courts. What Gandhi has said about the lawyers necessarily applies to the judges because they are first cousins and the one gives strength to the other.[38] Hence Gandhi asks the lawyers to give up his profession, and take up a handloom; devote his knowledge to enlightening both his people and the English, to refuse to be judge, and will not meddle with quarrels between parties."[39]

***(c)* Liberation for doctor** : According to Gandhi, the business of the doctor is really to rid the body of diseases but they interfere with the natural way of life and encourage us to break the laws of nature without impunity. They intervenes and donot allow nature to work. The result is loss of control over the mind. Doctors take to their profession not with a sense of serving humanity but to obtain honours and reaches.[40] So the doctors should give up medicine, and understand that rather than mending bodies, he should mend souls. Curing one disease by suppressing it through diabolical anti-biotic drugs and vivisection is invitingly a disease-nexus. He should tell the patients the cause of their diseases and will advise them to remove the cause rather than pamper them giving useless drugs.[41]

(d) **Liberation of the rich :** As Bible says that a camel can pass through the hole of a niddle but a rich man cannot go to heaven. Similarly, Gandhi feels that possession and happiness go ill together. Hence Gandhi's advice to them is to devote his money to establishing handlooms and commit no indulgence. He should know that we shall become free only through suffering.[42] Gandhiji felt that apart from the English language, the lawyer and the doctors, the rich people have been most responsible for encourages European civilization in India for which "even deportation for life to the Andamans is not enough expiation."[43] He should speak out his mind and fear no one and the last but not the least that he should not avoid any duty by saying that he shall do a thing when the others also do it.

Conclusion : Gandhiji had written *Hind Swaraj* after his tantalising experiments in South Africa and his life work in India is an unfoldment to follow the programme of action. So he said in 1921 : "I am individually working for the self rule pictured therein". It is *Hind Swaraj* which inspired him to cultivate fearlessness, non-violence and love and self-reliance and voluntary poverty. He fashioned his entire life in the light of the opinion expressed in *Hind Swaraj.* Being a Gujarati, he extensively used Hindustani, nay set up proganisations to propagate it. He abjured modern medicine and took to naturopathy. Though he used railways birthe travelled in third class. He gave up all his personal possessions. Through a network of constructive programmes, he taught and trained thousands of individuals to re-order their private lives according to the prescriptions in Hind Swaraj. He also set up scopes of organisations and institutions like all India Spinners Association, A.I. Harijan Sevak Sangh, A.I. Village Industries Association, A.I. Nai Talimi Sangh, A.I. Nature Cure Association, A.I. Prohibition Council and others to translate the values laid down in Hind Swaraj. Constructive Programmes aimed at creating "a new life style" and new organizational pattern. On the other hand, he spearheaded so many fighting programmes like Non-co-operation, Civil Disobedience etc. for achieving parliamentary *Swaraj* and for fighting injustice. In fact, Satyagraha and Constructive Programme proved to be a double-barrelled programme of action.

Hence when we are discussing Hind Swaraj, we must follow the logical corollary and go beyond. Unless it is followed up immediately by some programme of action (Whether it is civil obedience, non-cooperation and boycott or taking up constructive programme, a book like this would be rightly deemed as the product of a fossilised mind). That is why, we have said that Gandhism minus commitment is nothing. Hind Swaraj without Satyagraha and constructive programme is a crude Utopia. At individuals's point, such commitment would mean boycott of multinational consumer goods; opting for Swadeshi, boycott of five star hotels other vulgar show of wealth and minimising the use of English Language. The key to Hind Swaraj lies in action programmes.

REFERENCES

1. Gandhi, M.K., Hind Swaraj, Ahmedabad : Navajivan Publishing House, 1939 (Rev. New Edn), p. 110.
2. *Dictionary of Thought.*
3. Diwakar, R.R., *Samstha Kula*, Delhi, Raj Ghat, Vol. 18, No. 9, Dec. 1987, pp. 5-6.

4. In 1919 (after 10 years of publishing the book), he wrote to Maganlal, *Collected Works of Mahatama Gandhi,* Vol. 15, p. 340; In 1921 to the Critics, D.G. Tendulkar, *Mahatma,* Vol. 2, p. 17; In 1921, he wrote in the Foreword to the book, *Collected Works of Mahatma Gandhi,* Vol. 19. pp. 277-78; In March 1922 while commenting on a leaflet 'Gandhiraj'; in CWMG, Vol. 23, pp. 38-39; In 1924 at the time of undergoing operation on his appendicitis, CWMG, Vol. 23, p. 348; In 1929 in reply to SC Das Gupta, CWMG, Vol. 42, p. 125; In 1938, in *Aryan Path* (Special Number) CWMG, Vol. 67, pp. 169-70; In 1939 replying to a friend 'unbridegeable Gulf', CWMG, Vol. 70, p. 342; in Oct. 1939 talking to the Executive for Gandhi Seva Sangh, CWMG, Vol. 70, p. 296; on 14.6.'45 writing to Krishna Chandra, CWMG, Vo. 30, p. 325, last letter to Jawahar Lal Nehru, CWMG, Vol. 81, pp. 319-20.
5. CWMG, Vol. 24, p. 548.
6. CWMG, Vol. 42, p. 125.
7. CWMG, Vol. 67, p. 169-70.
8. CWMG, Vol. 80, p. 325.
9. CWMG, Vol. 81, p. 319.
10. Cloud, Preston, "Relation in Mineral Distribution", The Texas Quarterly, 1967.
11. Gawn, Sussane, *Moving Towards a New Society,* Philadelphia, 1976, pp. 64-65.
12. *Ibid.,* p. 89.
13. Capra, Fritjob, *The Turning Point : Science, Society and Rising Culture;* London, 1983, p. 3.
14. CWMG, Vol. 38, p. 243.
15. Gandhi, M.K., Hind Swaraj, What is True Civilization"?,
16. *Ibid.,* p. 61.
17. *Ibid.,* p. 62.
18. *Ibid.,* p. 62.
19. *Ibid.,* p. 62.
20. *Ibid.,* p. 63.
21. *Ibid.,* p. 8, Preface to the New Edition (Note by Mahadev Desai).
22. Devadutta, "Symposium on *Hind Swaraj*", Gandhi Marg, Oct. 1973, p. 267.

23. Diwakar, R.R., "Symposium on Hind Swaraj", *Ibid.*, p. 271.
24. Hind Swaraj, Preface to the New Edition (Note by Mahadev Desai), p. 9.
25. *Ibid.*, p. 9.
26. Aryan Path, Sept. 1938, p. 429.
27. Sant, Kishore "Gandhian Frame of Action", *Hind Swaraj : A Fresh Look* (ed.), N. Prasad, New Delhi : Gandhi Peace Foundation, 1985, p. 215.
28. Gandhi, M.K., *Hind Swaraj,* p. 101.
29. Sant, Kishore, *Ibid.*, p. 217.
30. Gandhi, M.K., *Hind Swaraj,* p. 10.
31. Gandhi, M.K., *Hind Swaraj,* p. 93.
32. Gandhi, M.K., *Young India,* 1.9.1921.
33. Gandhi, M.K., *Young India,* 21.4.1920.
34. Gandhi, M.K., *Hind Swaraj,* p. 102.
35. *Ibid.*, p. 54.
36. *Ibid.*
37. *Ibid.*, pp. 55-56.
38. *Ibid.*, p. 57.
39. *Ibid.*, (Item Nos. 2 to 5), p. 102.
40. *Ibid.*, p. 60.
41. *Ibid.*, (Item nos. 6,7,8), p. 102.
42. *Ibid.*, (Item Nos. 9-19), pp. 102-103.
43. *Ibid.*, p. 103.

6

Towards Economics of Swaraj

1. Total View of Human Life

To Gandhi, life is not like a water-tight compartment[1]. Hence it cannot be divided into social, political, economic etc. Thus he had an integral vision of man's life and society. Each aspect of life act and react upon each other. Hence any piecemeal study of Gandhian Economics is not only bound to create a partisan or partial view but also a distorted vision. Now it is high time to free oneself from the notion of one-dimensional man or the Economic Man and move towards the new horizon.

2. Gandhi as an Economist

It is no denying the fact that Gandhi was not an economist like Adam Smith, Marshall, Robins, Pigou, Keynes or even Marx. Nor he ever claimed it. Hence, J.B. Kripalani rightly said that "if there was a planner without elaborate blue-print, Gandhi was one of them".[2] Unlike other economists, Gandhi, he did not study economics academically. It was not in his nature too. He himself says, "I am not built for academic writings, Action is my domain".[3] He was not a theorist but primarily an activist. According to him, "solutions do not arise out of dogmatic, and doctrinaire approach but out of experience and struggle. Hence to borrow Toynbee's expression, Gandhi's economic ideas was "a response to challenge that poverty-ridden India flung to him".

3. Method

His method was to understand the scientific principles in the form of conditions that give rise to them. This means that in order to understand the economic problems we should see the conditions of the time[4]. It is why Gandhi studied in depth the impact of industrial revolution as well as modern civilization, which he has depicted in his *Hind Swaraj.* His method is therefore based on his experience and not on the basis of bookish knowledge. He saw the miserable conditions of the industrial labourers from India and other Asian countries brought to South Africa. Between 1550-1650, Black labour was used in mines in Bolivia in the most cruel and inhuman manner, so much so that the labourers were used in the 760 ft. deep in the mines for a week. Their average working life was therefore 3 to 4 months only. During 1500-1650, the Spanish colonialists, virtually looted 200 tons of gold worth 125 crores from the colonies. During 1800-1830, international trade increased from 30 crore sterling pound to 40 crores. Between 1840-70, it multiplied to 200 crore sterling pounds. Farmers too were exploited. Hence, we can easily understand new ways of plunder by World Bank, International Monetary Fund and the W.T.O. Western nations accumulated wealth through the worst forms of exploitation and because they combined trade with politics. All these provided Gandhi materials to express appropriate response to economics.

4. Concepts

However, Gandhi could discover the appropriate concepts of economics. But then, he did not treat them as absolve concepts but relative and without finality. He himself kept on elaborating, codifying, enriching the old context, as he was ever-growing. He grew from "truth to truth"[5]. His thoughts and ideas were never static but we cannot ever miss a direction in his fundamentals. He courageously ignored consistency in his earlier and later thoughts and allowed his readers to pick up his stand from his later writings if they differ from his earlier ones[6]. Like a scientist, he was in eternal quest of truth.

5. System without System-building

Like the classical and academic thinkers, hence he was not a absolutes or finalist which is the true spirit of a scientist. His "Collected Works" is a vast mass of materials spread over 7-8 decades, which have been skulled from different journals and papers and his speeches. There are hardly a few books, which he had the patience and time to write out like his *Autobiography* or *My Experiments with Truth, Satyagraha in South Africa* and *Hind Swaraj* (1909). But if we try to find out a system, we can have it from Dialectics to Dietectics, from Economics to Philosophy Politics to Sociology, Nature Cure to meditation, metaphysics to morals etc. In this way, he had a comprehensive vision and therefore an integral approach.

6. Forerunners of Gandhi's Ideas

Gandhi did not come out of vacuum. He inherited both his family-culture as well as the political-social culture of his time. In his family, he was influenced by his mother's life as a devout Vaishnaiva of the *Pranami-cult* which have taught to practice a life of purity, austerity and service. He was also influenced by the Jain doctrine of *non-possession* and limitation of wants. Similarly Buddha's life taught him to practice good to other following his doctrine of compassion. In the west, the life of Socrates and teachings of Lord Jesus had profound influences upon him. They inspired him to adopt a life of love and simplicity which were strengthened by Tolstoy concept of Bread Labour, Ruskin's emphasis upon dignity of labour and so on. John Ruskin's *Unto This Last* was a great critique of modern civilization and technology. Ruskin had challenged the very conception of modern economics and called it as a "dismal science of darkness" and more so as a "science of illth rather than wealth". *Ruskin's Unto This Last* became Gandhi's "Bible of Economics", where he got lessons in equality of wages for a band-labourer and a brain labourer." But he learnt the deep meaning of Ruskin's third principle that "the life of a manual labourer like the farmer is ideal" from Tolstoy. These two principles—equal wages of a brain-labourer and a hand-labourer and the preference of the like of physical labourer have radicalised Gandhi's economic thought by shunning elitism. The traditional economics, by recognising "organisation" and "enterprise" provided justification for both capitalism and social elitism. Even Marxism could not abolish the divide between the 'classes' and the 'masses' or through the concept of "burgeois" and the "proletariate", with the result there was at least 9 times inequality in the income in U.S.S.R. Gandhi by following Ruskin, has moved ahead towards equalisation in the economic and social fabric. Industrialisation and rapid introduction of high-technology has contributed in widening this divide. Hence, Gandhi introduced the principle of "Bread-labour" as one of his eleven vows. Social equality without economic equality or more so without the equality of wages cannot be achieved. Of course the various scriptures do mention about the equality of human beings, but it remained only spiritual idealism but Gandhi brought it at the level of social and organisational engineering. A small experiment of equal wages was introduced among all classes of Khadi workers in Bihar at the behest of Acharya Vinoba but the vested interests could not allow this system beyond two decades.

7. Some Basic Principles of Gandhi Economics

(a) **Meta-Economics of Mahatma Gandhi or Moral and Spiritual Approach to Economics :** Gandhi, like a rebel, challenged the very foundation of modern economics based upon "wealth" or "money". According to him, economics and ethics are vitally related. Economic order presupposes a social order which further involves a moral order also "True economics never militates against the highest ethical standard". An economics that inculcates Mammon worship and believes in the Darwinian doctrine of the survival of the fittest, is a dismal science which enables the strong to a mass at the expense of the weak. True, economics, therefore, stands for social and economic justice and universal welfare. Hence,

Gandhi never drew a sharp line of demarcation between economics and ethics. That economics is untrue which ignores or disregards moral values. Hence in his epoch making speech in 1916 at Muir College, Allahabad where he said that the scripture of the world are safer and sounder treatises on laws of economics than many modern text books. He (Jesus) is himself the greatest economist of his time"[7]. So Marshall's theory of demand and supply or Lord Keyane's theory of Liquidity Preference. Theory of Rate of Interest are neutral about the value judgement. It means that we should become rich even by exploitation and robbing others. If we follow the so-called Law of Demand and Supply bereft of moral compunction, some supplier might have created artificial scarcity to decrease the supply so that the price may increase. But this is bad economics equal to robbery.

***(b)* Economics of man** : Hence Gandhi propounded economics of man rather than an "enquiry into nature and causes of wealth of nations". Adam Smith put wealth in the forefront and man in the background. Hence writers like Carlyle, Ruskin or Gandhi condemned this mammon worship. Marshall improved this definition as "a study of man's action" and so did Robbins defined Economics as "study of human behaviour" but as a relationship between "scarce end and means" to get maximum material satisfaction. However the centre of Gandhian economic thought is "man", not "material prosperity". It is true, man cannot live without bread but this is also true that he cannot live with bread alone. Hence Gandhi takes a totalistic view of happiness because like Wordsworth, he was true to the kindred points of heaven and earth. He did understand the importance of material necessities and comforts of life but he did not stop there and took adequate note of psychological and spiritual aspects of human life.

***(c)* Economics of Permanence** : However, he was not in favour of an unbridled consumerism. There can be use and misuse of his free will. By wrong use of will, man displaces this natural function by allaying his thirst with ever increasing wants. "Nature has enough to meet his needs but not his greed", says Gandhi. This has caused both ecological and social problems like parasitic Economy and an unscientific exploitation of nature. Hence Gandhi advocated an Economy of Permanence and Sustainable Development. There are two models of development—1. Transient-Destructive and 2. Permanent-Creative. The first is based on 'Rights' with the absence of altruistic values. There are three stages of them *(a)* Parasitic Economy *(b)* Economy of Perdition and *(c)* Economy of Enterprise. The second model is that of Economy of Gregation and Economy of Service. In short, this is Economy of Values. In fact, this is the Economy of Permanence. Unless we put a control upon our desires and wants, we shall have to exploit nature as cruelly as possible leading to the rapid erosion of natural wealth as well as environmental problems. We have seen the dreadful reports of the Club of Rome. There has been rape of the earth, water and other natural resources. Due to extreme pollution, there have been dangerous holes in the ozone and even acid rains. The threat of nuclear holocaust is also there. Hence, we have to limit our craze for over consumerism. Due to brutal exploitation of nature, we have already exhausted coal, petrol etc. There is water-crisis in the offing. Hence, use must return to less and less consumption not as a spiritual demand but as our compulsion. Our emphasis upon limitation of wants or a sort of voluntary poverty if not wantlessness is the demand of the time.

***(d)* Economics of peace :** Peace is not only an absence of war. There are good structural causes of violence like poverty, unemployment, wrong use of political power and social injustices etc. Not only this, even inequality breeds violence. Hence Gandhi through his gospel of work, decentralisation and small and cottage industries tried to achieve social peace. Violence is ingrained in a centralised economy.

Large-scale industries need large capital, big technology and bigger markets which are bound to create fierce and unhealthy competition and consequently war. It was Great

Britain, France, Spain etc. who practiced cut throat competition for capturing market. This involved big and small wars. Hence industrialization brought an economy of war. Today arms and ammunition worth over 10 thousand billion dollars are manufactured every year and sold mostly to Asian and African countries, while the masses remain hungry, half clad and illiterate.

***(e)* Economics of High Technology : Industrialization :** Industrial Revolution, no doubt, came as a blessing. We learnt "to ride the waves of the wind, to harness the rivers, watering deserts, to master the earth and the creatures thereof and with the earth as our foot stool reach out to the stars"[9] but today it has become a curse. Even western thinkers like Tolstoy categorized the grave evils of machinery and industrial civilization. Gandhi was very critical of industrial civilization for exploitation, alienation, and dehumanization of man. He did not want large-scale production but production by the masses : Then decentralisation and non-violence go together. In fact, Gandhi was not against machinery as such. He advocated appropriate technology. For example, a big country like India with a big population but small capital, small-scale industries are more suitable to ease unemployment and under-employment. That use of machinery is lawful, moral and practical "which subserves the interest of all"[10]. Hence he is on record to say that he would favour the use of the "most elaborate machinery if thereby India's pauperism and resulting idleness is avoided " Gandhi would distinguish between machine and machine. For example he is totally against those machines which produce arms and armaments for the destruction of mankind. Similarly, he is also again the use of those machines, which create unemployment. But he is in favour of these machines which provide employment and removes human drudgery etc. He is also critical of industrial civilization as it has created unmanageable and unwieldy cities, consumerism, pollution and a culture of exploitation, crime and corruption. So his picture of Swaraj is the picture of a small but beautiful habitation where people have got some employment and live in peace and harmony.

(f) **Economic of Swadeshi & Swaraj :** Swaraj is not only freedom from foreign rule. It is not simply political freedom. National independence go along with national self-reliance or Swaraj. He was in favour of freedom of Self and also of the nation. What to speak of our sovereignty, even our democracy, our culture and our life-styles are not safe under economic dependence. However, this is not possible without self-reliance and Swadeshi. Swadeshi must not be misconstrued in the narrow sense of national chauvinism. We must admit that only a tree, independent and self-sufficient India can serve the world. But his patriotism is not exclusive, it is not only not to hurt another nation but to benefit all in the true sense of the word. Hence Gandhi clearly said "India's freedom as conceived by me can never be a menace to the world"[12]. Freedom is our birth right but non-exploitation of other countries is our most sacred duty. Hence the modern slogan of globalisation is not an anathema but unfortunately it is retrial of liberalisation, privatisation and exploitation by three capitalist agencies of World Bank, International Monetary Fund and World Trade Organization. The first era of so called globalisation started in 1890-1913, the second phase during 1950-1980 and the third phase of globalisation came in 1980 with high-technology. It is neither universalism nor liberalism. It is pure a corporate scheme of the vested interest for the purpose of exploitation of the developing countries and with the veiled purpose of political dominance in the world-politics. Economically, it creates "Jobless growth", poverty, insecurity in the developing countries, hence violence and anarchy have increased while world output growth has dropped by 2%, world trade has diminished in the Asian-African countries. The so called Asian Tigers, which were show pieces of models of 'globalisation' turned to Pusy Cats during the depression and the masters had to rush with massive loan to save their edifice from crumbling and collapse. Even in U.S.A. in 2003 there were 40 million people below poverty line. In India, during this period of so-called economic reforms, the world trade has gone down from 195.59 lakhs in 1997 to 191.38 lakhs in 2001. So it is a myth that globalisation

creates economic progress. Even it creates wealth, it is usurped by only 20% of the population. This is because the economic planning in India has ignored the critical question of demographic and social factor in the development.

Apart from these glaring economic defects, there are serious political drawbacks also. Western nations have accumulated wealth while the third-world countries have lost. On the other hand, W.T.O. has invaded upon human rights and even constitutional rights of these countries under pretext of international agreement. There has been weakening of labour unions; world monopoly through Patent laws and farmers' exploitation by compelling them to purchase seeds, manures and pesticides from them. There has been very ugly interference with the sovereignty of nations like Brazil, Bolivia etc. On social plane, the entire world has been turned into a big market where corruption, addiction, blackmarketing, criminalisation and vulgar consumerism abound. There has been no guarantee of job in a factory and with no human dignity.

"Poorna Swaraj means full economic freedom for the toiling millions. It is no unholy alliance with any interest for their exploitation"[13] It is complete freedom from alien yoke in every sense of the term and this is for the sake of dumb millions[14]. Hence Swaraj is impossible with Swadeshi. But there are *true* as well as *false* Swadeshi. Any article is Swadeshi if it subserves the interests of the million, even though the capital and talent may be all foreign but under effective Indian control. It means that Swadeshi should not be made a fetish. To reject foreign, and to go on wasting national time and energy will be a criminal folly.[16] In fact he want rational and balanced Swadeshi.

(g) **Economics of Bread Labour :** According to traditional Economics, there are four factors of production—land, labour, capital and organization. We can add even enterprise as the fifth one. But, there has been a chasm between the physical labour and the mental labour with superiority and prestige

given to brain-labourer. Although the scriptures like the Bible and the Gita do eulogise the dignity of labour but in common use there is difference between the 'wages' of a labourer and 'salary' of a supervisor or manager. But Gandhi did not want to discriminate between the two as the theory of Bread Labour was both a philosophy and economics to Gandhi—"That to live man must work". This idea came to Gandhi first from reading Tolstoy, then from Ruskin's *Unto This Last*. However, this was first stressed by a Russian writer named T.M. Bondaref and also in the 3rd chapter of the Gita—"He who eats without offering sacrifices eat stolen food."[17] According to Gandhi, the violation of this principle is the root cause of economic disequilibrium. He regards it as a natural law binding on all. It is compulsory duty. Its neglect creates social division between the Elites and the Proletariates. Gandhi's insistence is enforced by the Bible—"In the sweat of thy brow thou shalt eat thy bread". A millionaire cannot carry on for long, and will soon get tired of his life, if he rolls in his bed all day along, and is even helped to his food. He, therefore, induces hunger by taking exercise. Even from social standpoint, a worldwide conflict between capital and labour, and the poor envy the rich, if all worked for their bread, distinctions of rank would be obliterated. This might be unattainable ideal, but we need not cease to strive for it. A question arises—May not men earn their livelihood by intellectual labour? The answer is : The needs of the body must be supplied by the body. Render unto Caesar which is the so called economic reforms in the name of LPG have failed to remove poverty of the masses and unemployment. There is jobless growth. Marxism also failed to remove inequality and instead deprived us of our liberty and individual freedom. Even mixed economy could not also succeed. Hence we have to find out a system which would guarantee individual freedom and economic prosperity. Modern economists have no answer as to what would be appropriate institutional set up for combining economic efficiency and individual freedom.

Here Gandhi provides Trusteeship model which is India's

gift to the world. Here not only the capital is socialised but labour has also been socialised. He brought ethics to Economics and gave dignity to the rich by making them trustees. They would give up private ownership of their property and create out of it a trust valid in the eyes of the law court and managed democratically. Trusteeship provides a means of transformation. The present capitalist order of security into an egalitarian one. It gives no quarter to capitalise but gives the present owning class a chance of reforming itself. It is based on the faith that human nature is never beyond redemption. But it does not recognise any right of private ownership of property except it may be permitted by society. It does not recognise right of inheritance also. It does not exclude legislated regulation of the ownership and use of wealth. Thus under state regulated ownership, an individual will not be free to hold or use his wealth for selfish reason or in disregard of the interest of society. There are the six points of Trusteeship Theory presented by Prof. M.L. Dantwala and approved by Gandhiji.[18] Business is so inextricably woven in the very texture of society that it is inalienable from it. The relation between business and society may be based either on conflict or cooperation. If the private sector realise they have their part as trustees, there is really Ramrajya. Gandhi wanted to take advantage of the skill of the business people devoid of dirty profiteering and black-marketing etc.

To say that such an idea is not practicable, is natural but one should try to learn from the experiments of Gandhi in South Africa and by some other people elsewhere. There may of suitable legislation and finally Mahatma's weapons of non-cooperation and Satyagraha are there. Vinoba had shown that lakhs of acres of land may be donated to the landless and Gramdan is a kind of trusteeship experiment. When capitalism and class war both are despicable trusteeship is the hope for future. E.F. Schumacher has also expressed that "if India should be able to move along the path of equality through trusteeship, she would be a beacon to the world". The success lies in experimentation as both systems of capitalism and socialism have failed.

8. Conclusion

Gandhian Economics is not based on rigid doctrinaire approach, it is based on common sense experience. It has faith in the goodness of man and his rationality. Its goal is welfare not of one section of society but of all. Hence it is not sectional or sectarian. Hence there is least chance of conflict. Similarly, the means are also different *i.e.,* love and non-violence. Hence it is a viable alternative before the world. Gandhi has demonstrated the efficacy of love and non-violence in the field of economics Vinobaji has tried to show the path. But if we do not wish to take the prescribed means and medicines and simply try to accuse that it is utopian or unpractical, we must face the music of violence, terrorism and bloody revolution. Let economists and thinkers leave the beaten track and think courageously. It is not Utopian but pragmatic, it is not based on ivory-tower but practical and realistic. Lousi Fischer wrote—"If man is to survive, if civilization is to survive and flower in freedom, truth and democracy the remainder of the 20th century and what lies beyond must belong not to Lenin or Trotsky, nor to Marx or Mao or Ho-chi Minh but to Mahatma Gandhi". I would like to add that L.P.G. or the so called globalism cannot save humanity. We require globalism of Mahatma Gandhi with no war, no conquest, no exploitation. We want freedom from want but also limitation of our wants, not unbriddled liberalisation, to save the humanity and our civilization.

REFERENCES

1. Gandhi, 'M.K., *Selection from (Gandhi,* ed. N.K. Bose, Ahmedabad; Navajivan Prakashan, 1948, *Young India,* 2.3.22.
2. Kripalani, J.B., *Gandhi : His Life and Thought,* Calcutta : Orient Longmans, 1961, p. 262.
3. *Harijan : A* Journal of Applied Gandhism, 1933-55, New York, 3.1.46, p. 28.
4. Bhattacharya, B., *Evolution of the Political Philosophy of Mahatma Gandhi,* Calcutta : Indian Associated Publishing Co., 1940, p. 32.

5. *Harijan,* 29.4.1934, p. 260.

6. *Harijan,* 29.4.1933, p. 2.

7. *Collected Works of Mahatma Gandhi,* Vol. XIII, pp. 311-17.

8. Adam Smith, *An Essay on the Nature and Causes of Wealth of Nations,* New York, The Modern Library, 1937.

9. Radhakrishnan, S., *Speeches and Writings,* Third Series, New Delhi : Publications Division, Govt. of India, 1959-62.

10. Gandhi, M.K., Young India, 15.4.26.

11. *Ibid.,* 3.11.21.

12. Gandhi, M.K., *Young India,* 3.4.24.

13. Gandhi, M K., *Young India,* 16.4.31.

14. Gandhi, M.K., *Young India,* 17.9.31.

15. Gandhi, M.K., *Harijan,* 25.2 39.

16. Gandhi, M.K., From *Yarvada Mandir,* p. 85.

17. Gandhi, M.K., Bhagvad Gita, III. 12 *cp. Manu Smrti* III.76, 118.

18. Upadhyaya, R.B., *Social Responsibility of Business and Trusteeship Theory of M.K. Gandhi,* p. 71.

7

Swaraj, Swadeshi and One World

"Swaraj is our birth-right"—said Lokmanya Tilak. "As every country is fit to eat, to drink and to breathe, even so is every nation fit to manage its own affairs, no matter how badly"[1]—said Gandhiji. Gandhiji further elaborated the concept of Swaraj and he said that "mere withdrawal of the English is not independence. It means the consciousness in the average villager that he is the maker of his own destiny, he is his own legislator through his chosen representatives."[2] He neither wanted to copy the British Parliamentary system nor the Soviet, the Fascist or Nazi rule. He wanted *Ramraj i.e.,* "sovereignty of the people based on pure moral authority."[3] The Swaraj of his dream is "the poor man's Swaraj"....The necessaries of life should be enjoyed by you in common with those enjoyed by the princes and monied men... I have not the slightest doubt that Swaraj is not *Purna Swaraj* untill these amenities are guaranteed to you under it."[4] It recognises "no race or religious distinction. Nor is it to be the monopoly of the latter persons nor yet of monied men. Swaraj is to be for all, including the former, but emphatically including the maimed, the blind, the starving, toiling millions."[5] Gandhiji was not interested in freeing India from merely the English yoke. "I am bent upon freeing India from any yoke whatsoever, I have no desire to exchange "king log for king stork". Hence for me the movement of Swaraj is a movement of self-purification."[6] Swaraj can never be a free gift by one nation to another. It is a treasure to be purchased with a nation's best blood. "Swaraj will be the fruit of incessant labour, suffering beyond measure."[7]

However, Gandhi's "nation of Purna Swaraj is not isolated independence but healthy and dignified interdependence."[8] His nationalism, fierce tough it is, is not exclusive, not designed to harm any nation or individual. It can be no peril to other nations. "Through Swaraj we would serve the whole world."[9] His non-cooperation was neither with the English nor with the West but with the system the English had established, with the material civilization and its attended greed and exploitation of the weak.

This only means that "we must refuse to be lifted off our feet. A drawning man cannot save ourselves... India must learn to live before she can aspire to die for humanity."[10] He would like to see India free and strong so that "she may offer herself as a willing and pure sacrifice for the betterment of the world."[11] Gandhi had forseen the aspirations for a "world community" or "one world". According to him "the better mind of the world desires today not absolutely independent States warring one against another but a federation of friendly interdependent States." He was expressing his readiness "for universal interdependence rather than independence."[12] He agreed that in these days of rapid intercommunication and growing consciousness of oneness of all mankind, "our nationalism must not be inconsistent with progressive internationalism."[13] We cannot stand in isolation and unaffected by what is going on in other parts of the world. "A truly independent India is bound to run to the help of its neighbours in distress."[14] In short, Indian nationalism is not exclusive, not aggressive nor destructive. It is health-giving, religious and therefore humanitarian. The Indian moral maxim rightly says, "sacrifice our personal interest for the family; the latter for the village; the village for the district; the district for the province; the province for the nation; the nation for all."

Hence, there is no conflict with *globalism* and *Swadeshi,* because Swadeshi was the spirit which dictated man to serve his next door neighbour to the exclusion of any other. Besides, "neighbour thus served had in turn to serve his own neighbour. In this sense, Swadeshi was never exclusive. "It simply recognised the scientific limitation of human capacity for service."[15] He said with pride that he lived for India's freedom and would die for it. He worked for India's freedom because his *Swadeshi* taught him that being born in it and having inherited her culture, he was fittest to serve her and Mother India had a prior claim to his service. But he said : "my patriotism is not exclusive, it is calculated not only to hurt another nation but to benefit all in the true sense of the world." India's freedom as conceived by me can never be a menace to the world."[16] He did not want freedom of his country at the expense or exploitation of others or to degrade other countries. His idea of nationalism is that "my country may become free, that if need be, the whole country may lie, so that the human race may live."[17]

Similarly, Swadeshi principle of planning in India would not introduce schemes of industrializing the country for the maximum utilisation of her raw materials, and not of her abundant and unused man-power which is left to take care of itself as best as it can. Gandhi never considered Swadeshi as a *fetish*, or "the exclusion of everything foreign under every conceivable circumstance." The broad definition of Swadeshi is "the use of all home-made things to the exclusion of foreign things, in so far as such use is necessary for the protection of home industry, more especially those industries without which India will be pauperized."[18] He warned that "like any good thing, even *Swadeshi*, can be ridden to death if it is made a fetish.[19] Gandhi differentiated between a 'true Swadeshi' and a 'false Swadeshi'. "Any article is Swadeshi if it serves the interest of the millions, even though the capital and talent are foreign but under effective Indian control." Conversely, "Bata's shoes would be *foreign* though the labour employed may be all Indian and the capital also found by India. The manufactures will be doubly foreign because the control will be in foreign hands and the article, no matter how cheap it is, will oust the village tanner mostly and the village *mochi* always."[20]

Swadeshi also means self-respect with a moral dimension.

In concrete terms, it can today, at best mean that we produce goods that can stand up to goods produced in any developed country in terms of quality; we try and export more than we import and that we provide social security to our poor neighbours and countrymen by mobilising our own resources. Swadeshi has not come with Gandhiji. Earlier Dada Bhai Naoroji and Tilak had talked about it. There was a positive and moral aspect as we were under British rule. Today, our campaign looks somewhat negative and contradictory. For example can we talk of EEC, SAARC, ASEAN, etc. and pure *Swadeshi* in the same breath? Can we morally justify that a Birla or a Tata should be free to set up industry in Nigeria, Kenya but a Swiss or French firm cannot do so in India? This moral dilemma comes before only we forget the Gandhian Principles of Swadeshi which is based on the spirit of both 'neighbourhood' as well as 'one world'.

In the narrow sense, Swadeshi means an economic process in which there is a pronounced preference for, a clearly specified bias in favour of home produced goods and services, locally available capital; enterprise and labour as against foreign imported goods and services, technologies and techniques, capital enterprise and labour. Absolute Swadeshi would not bother about comparative costs; in specialisation and trade or to differences in relative factor endowments in different countries. "Such a concept of Swadeshi" says Dr. P.R. Brahmanand "would become close to autarchy."[21]

The Mahalanobis model of Swadeshi emphasised eventually complete self-reliance in respect of all heavy industry products and their accessories including the technological sources. But in an international context, such a model has hardly any rational justification. Lest Swadeshi should not become a fetish, it should mean that the model of development, would be as to make available consumption goods at comparatively cheaper costs to consumers. But this should satisfy two conditions—*(i)* Maximum employment prospects are available to the countrymen and, *(ii)* from the balance of payments angle, exports should pay for imports and there should be no exploitation, in terms of one-way drain.

Now let us briefly examine the present economic scenario with the tests, of utilitarianism—its effect on the *last man*, the rural population, the population dependent on small scale and cottage industries, economy in public expenditure, ethical standards permeated economic behaviours, the extent by which income and consumption disparities were getting reduced and so on. It is clear that Gandhiji would not have in favour of inflationary processes for these would discriminately hurt large masses of population, especially in rural areas and engaged in small and cottage industries, where income is not indexed—linked with respect to inflation. He would not have liked reducing the growth rate of employments or ordinary labour in the unorganised sector. He would have never liked speculative activities which are never sympathetic to the poor people and increasing their expenditure and consumption patterns. He would have been against monopolistic practices emanating either from employers organizations or trade unions. On the contrary, he would have favoured organisations of consumers to protect themselves against exploitation. He would have been against excessive wage increases as also of excessive profit accruals. Reduction in govt. expenditure and check on permissiveness in the write offs policies regarding bank loans would have been his high priorities.

Besides, economic utility, Gandhi had also some moral imperatives, like austerity and simple living, which had nothing to do with higher rates of growth or higher forms of material satisfaction. Similarly, his concern for the village self-sufficiency, trusteeship, human technology and concern for environment and ecology were his guiding values. It is wrong to think that development is not possible in Swadeshi-model. If it were so, how could Korea, Taiwan and Japan develop to such an extent, though their economies had considerable Swadeshi-content, self-reliance and growth? Vietnam is far ahead of India in inviting foreign direct investment which has still a Communist Government. So in China, the volume of foreign investment is perhaps 30 to 50 times more than

India. We can note Gandhi's advice of rigorous self-control in tackling the population problem. But if we cannot practice self-control, how can we oppose birth-control? But this does not take away moral base of self-control. Similarly, we may not accept the concept of village self-sufficiency in an interdependent world but this does-not-take away Gandhian value of village life and its self-sufficiency because even now India lives in villages. The key is not to take Gandhiji literally. If unbridled acquisitiveness and material employment go on and there is no discipline, wrong priorities, and blind devotion after big technology continue the so-called new economic policy cannot succeed. Hence a Gandhian self-discipline and austerity, adoption of appropriate technology and right priorities are essential.

We have regressed from 'self-reliance to 'self-sufficiency'. Self-sufficiency as a temporary phenomena might be useful but as a permanent economic doctrine it is dangerous. There is no conflict between Swadeshi and internationalism. We have to recognise the limits of each. Swadeshi asks to act locally but to think globally. Like Wordsworth's Skylark, Swadeshi is true to the kindred points of world-fraternity and utmost concern for our immediate neighbour. It is not for nothing that Jesus ordained : "Love thy neighbours". "Swadeshism is not the cult of hatred. It is a doctrine of selfless service that has its roots in the purest *ahimsa, i.e. love.*"[22] It is consistent with the law of humanity and love.[23] "I must not serve distant neighbour at the expense of the nearest".[24] He further says : "I refuse to buy from anybody anything however nice or beautiful if it interferes with my growth or injures those whom Nature has made my first care."[25] India must protect her primary industries even as a mother protects her children against the whole world without being hostile to it.[26]

Swadeshi is not a national chauvinism, it is "a message to the world".[27]

REFERENCES

1. *Young India,* 15.10.1931.
2. *Ibid.,* 13.2.1930.
3. *Harijan,* 2.1.1937.
4. Y.I., 26.3.1931.
5. Y.I., 3.9.1925.
6. Y.I., 12.6.1924.
7. Y.I., 5.1.1922.
8. Y.I., 26.3.1931.
9. Y.I., 16.4.1931.
10. Y.I., 13. 10. 1921.
11. Y.I., 17.9.1925.
12. Y.I., 26.10.1924.
13. *Amrit Bazar Patrika,* 17.9.33.
14. *Harijan,* 23.3.1947.
15. *Ibid.*
16. Y.I., 3.4.1924.
17. *Collected Works of Mahatma Gandhi,* Vol. IV, p. 170.
18. *Young India,* 17.6.1926.
19. From *Yarvada Mandir,* p. 95.
20. *Harijan,* 25.2.1939.
21. Brahmanand, P.R., "What would Gandhiji Have Thought About Us and Our Economy?" *Swadeshi,* (ed.) S.V. Raju, Bombay, 1994, p. 2.
22. Gandhi, M.K., quoted in *The Mind of Mahatma* (ed.) Prabhu & Rao (Publications Division, New Delhi), 3rd ed. 1968, p. 415.
23. *Ibid.,* p. 412.
24. *Complete Works of Mahatma Gandhi,* Vol. XXVI, p. 278.
25. *Ibid.*
26. *Ibid.,* Vol. XXV, p. 369.
27. Tendulkar, D.G., *Mahatma,* Delhi : Publications Division, 2nd ed. 1960, Vol. 2, p. 64.

8

Swaraj and Global Democracy

In spite of defects and deficiencies in formal and structural conditions of modern democratic set up, there is no substitute for democracy except a better and improved version. Global democracy is inseparable from global polity—World Government, Global Pedagogy and a just Economic Order.

Pre-condition

Present day democracy is more formal than real. It is understood as a form of government and not as a philosophy of life. It is regarded as a purely political problem and not as a socio-cultural as well as an ethical problem. We often become undemocratic in our behaviour as we do not have conviction and commitment to the moral democratic values. Hence it has been reduced to a political tool. Of course, we can raise meta-ethical questions as to why we should be moral or ethical. We have to be ethical because we live in human society where we do not have the monopoly to do what we like. Thus polity is essentially rooted in morality and democracy, and is essentially a moral and ethical phenomenon. It is an ingredient of social organizations. We need a good polity and this presupposes faith in the essential goodness of man. On the contrary, if we regard that man is essentially brute and evil, it is not only an insult to the entire humanity but it is also a message of pessimism par excellence. Hence any idea of democracy should have faith in essential goodness of man.

Whether democracy is local, national, or global, it rests on the basic postulate that man is essentially good. With the complexity of social and political problems in modern times, the struggle for existence has become more and more acute and there is a strong tendency to grab more and more powers in political and/or economic affairs. According to Toffler, power wealth and knowledge are the three major aspirations of human life. The moral problems are bound to emerge out of the vortex of socio-political problems. That is why we are facing crisis after crisis in our political life. In fact, we are living in sick societies. Our democracy and polity have been facing serious predicaments. Therefore, a good society is a pre-conditions for a good polity, successful parliamentary democracy and party system.

Our parliamentary system of democracy is more formal and much less real as the very structure of our democratic system suffers from structural and other weaknesses. In a democracy, people are sovereign. However, power lies with the party, party bosses and party caucuses in the party based parliamentary democracy as the real control rests with the parties. Thus, power ultimately goes to the party rulers, and hence there is an element of negation of people's power. Policy making, selection of the candidates for elections, preparing the budget and conducting the affairs of the government rests with a small group of party bosses. People are not aware of the major changes in policies regarding economy, finance, trade, commerce, foreign affairs, science, technology, space and nuclear issues and other important and highly specialized things. In short, Party dictatorship prevails in the name of democracy. The system of democracy is formal but not real in many countries. The dictators have emerged out of the party system mechanism even in our times, such as Hitler in Germany. Recently, the military rulers in Pakistan and Indira Gandhi in India had usurped all powers to become dictators with the sanction of there respective parliaments. So, Gandhi openly and bluntly said that the western (parliamentary) democracy is only formal which means that it grants political rights but neglects the economic rights of people. The charter of fundamental rights does not mention the crucial "Right to

Work". All other rights lose their importance because economy is the basis for existence of life. Hence, Political democracy looses its luster without economic democracy.

It is pointed out by communists that they do not have multi-party system but they have right to work enshrined in their Constitution. They also deny the so called freedom of having many parties because the party is a part of class and the class is primarily, of peasants and workers. Therefore there is only one party, the Communist Party, the vanguard of people. They claim to have peoples' democracy in the real sense. Although we cannot deny the merit of emphasizing economic democracy and economic equality; we know that in the name of dictatorship of the proletariat, there has been autocracy, and hence the concept of Glasnost & Perestroika has been advanced. The communist party has itself become a privileged class with vested interests. The so called peoples' democracy turns anti-democratic.

Nationalism as the Negation of Global Democracy

Nationalism has been a sacred cult based on patriotism in human history. It played a great role in librating worn out system in human history, *i.e.* the system of feudalism. But now nationalism has become the cult of tribalism. Nearly seven thousand wars have been fought in the name of nationalism during the last seven thousand years and it is going on endlessly even now.

The 20th century has seen two World Wars and the dropping of deadliest atom bombs on Hiroshima and Nagasaki. The nationalism has proved to be dangerous for the entire human civilization. In fact, global democracy is unthinkable without a world government and a global society. Socrates had said—"I am neither an Athenian nor a Greek but a citizen of the world." Wendell Wilkie had advocated about a world government in his book "One World." Alfred Toynbee, Swietzer and others have already pleaded for world polity. Gandhi had gone much ahead of his time when he said that he would not like to live "if it is not one world". The Indian concept to treat the whole world as one family is reflected in Sanskrit verse, Vasudhaiva Kutumbkam".. In short, we must strive for a world government and a world citizenship for global democracy.

Global Religion

Religion has been damned as the opium of the people by Marx and Engles but even the great Indian Vedantic Swami Vivekananda and others have decried the harmful role of various sectarian religions. In the world nearly six thousand small and big bloody battles have been fought in the name of religions. In Christianity alone there is a record of hundred years of war between the Catholics and the Protestants. The Middle-East countries and the Indian sub-continent have been facing the worst hysteria of religious fundamentalism. If the west has invented the Atom Bomb the religious fanatics have also practiced Human Bombs. It is necessary to have Universal Religion in place of personal and sectarian religions. We cannot deny that religions have got many blessings and they are strong forces of our social and cultural life. They do influence our political life and democratic structure hence the ideal of Universal Religion (Vivekananda) and Principle of Equal Respect for All Religions (Gandhi) or Religion of Man (Tagore) should underlie the basis of our religious faiths. To regard one's own religion as the best or the finest necessarily implies that all religions other than ours are inferior. This is sacrilege and anti democratic.

Gender Democracy

According to Engels, the first form of social exploitation was the exploitation of women by men. This statement has element of truth because the patriarchal system has been in force throughout the world after the primitive communism. Men have got control over property and social organizations and brutal discrimination against women continued during the long strides of human civilization. Even the advanced democratic countries like UK did not grant women the right to vote till late in the 19th century. I have not heard of any woman occupying the post of high priest like the Pope in the west and the heads of religious orders in the east. The cruelest system of burning the widows after the death of her husband, like "sati" system and many other acts of repression and oppression continue in the 21st century also. Women are generally not responsible for war, violence and crime. Hence, it is necessary to awaken the potential power of the matriarchal society to share the economic, social, political and cultural leadership proportionately. I am sure; a global democracy needs not only a global awareness but also an awareness of equality of men and women.

Non-Violence for Global Democracy

Democracy is applied non-violence in politics hence violence and democracy cannot go together. Imperialist powers have been fighting for the expansion of their empire in the whole world. Great Britain along with her allies did not hesitate to invade Suez. US President Bush attacked Afghanistan and then Iraq and the war is not over even now. The communist country, Russia had trampled over freedom of Czechoslovak and Hungry. Peoples' Republic of China also fought a war against communist Vietnam. India, the land of Buddha and Gandhi has the fourth largest land army with atom bombs. We are living in world of war and terror which can wipe out the entire human existence. There are more than thirty thousand hydrogen bombs in the world. If there is an atomic war, the entire human civilization will be annihilated, hence we have to choose between Atom Bomb and Non-violence. If we cannot abolish war, war will itself abolish us. "Similarly if we cannot abolish structural violence (domestic violence, campus violence, cast, communal, regional and linguistic violence, criminal violence, state violence and so called revolutionary violence) we cannot think of a democratic social and political order.

In fact this is a charter for a long march for establishing a world government, a universal religion and a world free from violence.

9

Hind Swaraj and Peace

Peace is perhaps the most desirable ideal of human civilisation. However, the term peace is given to different meanings and interpretations. For the spiritualists, it means internal peace of mind and soul, without which we cannot achieve happiness and bliss. Hence the Gita clearly says that without peace, happiness is impossible. To the Buddhists, the supreme state of bliss called Nibaan is the state of peace and tranquility, which is described as tranquil like the sea or the Jain concept of Moksha is also similar. Even the Nyaya-Vaisesika concept of Moksha tends towards defining peace as a state of utter tranquility and bliss. In the Sankhya philosophy, the highest state is described as the state of supernegation as 'nothing is mine', I am not a thing (ना मे अस्मि), I am not (Na Asmi) and I am not an individual (Na Aham-I am not the ego). In the eight fold path of yoga, the highest state is that of Samadhi, which is the state of super consciousness. In the Advaita Vedanta, the highest wisdom consists in the identification of the self with the Absolute or subject as the object (Tattvamasi—Thou art that or I am Brahman (अहं ब्रह्म अस्मि)—which is the state of super tranquility and peace. In short, the highest state of spirituality is the state of internal peace and tranquility. Apart from Indian philosophy, even in different religious philosophies, we have almost a common emphasis upon internal peace apart from peace as a moral and spiritual phenomenon. Hence, almost all religions of the world have univocally and unconditionally advocated the concept of peace.

To the Jews, it is 'Shalom' or grace flowing from the heaven', to the Semitic fathers, it is 'The blessing Justice of God'. The Roman peace (PAX) is different. It means a tranquil harmony "within the hierarchy of heaven; To The Hindus, the Vedic term 'Shanti' is a prayer of peace universal-light, earth, water, vegetable, kingdom, medicines and all others. In Islam, the word Salam means 'peaceful acceptance' of God, calm resignation or total surrender to the will of God. The Chinese, Huo' Ping means "Smooth or tranquil harmony within the hierarchy of heaven.

After pursuing the different meanings of peace in different metaphysical and religious systems, I am constrained to believe that peace is regarded mostly as air internal affair, which is also justified because unless we have peace within, we cannot think of peace without or outside ourselves. However, this is a tragic evidence of history that during the last 7000 years of religious history of mankind, at least 6,500 small and big religious wars have taken place. Even Christianity has witnessed 100 years of war between the Catholics and Protestants. The sword of Islam has had reached upto Spain and even now in the middle East there has been a savage fighting between the Islamic countries and Israel. Even the Hindus have not been a peaceful, social and religious system. In short, the record of religions has been seriously unfortunate. This is why, Marx has dubbed religion as an 'opium of the people'. It is therefore, that there has been religions reformers of humanists and cosmopolitan outlook almost in all religions. In modern times, Swami Vivekanand has advocated the cause of 'universal religion', Tagore has emphasised upon 'religion of man' and Gandhi has adhered to the doctrine of equal respect for all religions.

Many scholars like Dr. Bhagwan Das and other Theosophists have dwelt upon the idea of essential unity of all religions. In the western world, there has been no dearth of such persons spousing the cause of world religion along with the concept of world government. If we cannot mend the sectarian cult of religions in the religious orders, there is no other way than to end it. As we have learnt the doctrine of co-existence in world politics and international affairs, it is necessary to understand the value of co-existence in all religions. If one thinks that his religion alone is the best or most superior, it naturally implies that religions of others than ours are inferior and downgraded. This is a very unhealthy frame of mind based on jealousy and ill-will.

There is another important cause of global violence based on the prevalent doctrine of narrow nationalism. No doubt, patriotism is a noble human sentiment and nationalism had come as a safety valve against sectarian feudalism during the 17th and 18th centuries. People were the feudal Lords where they fought like tribal chiefs waging most cruel warfare but today nationalism has assumed the same tribal outlook and they have made the entire human civilisation as unsafe and insecure. Not less than 7000 wars have been fought in the name of nationalism during human history. Even our modern 20th century has witnessed the horrors of two world wars and also dropping of deadly nuclear weapons upon Hiroshima and Nagasaki. Even the 21st century has been face to face most dangerous and inhuman acts of terrorism and human bombs. Needless to say, that there is a dangerous stockpile of 30,000 dreadful nuclear bombs stored in the nuclear Arsenals and if by chance due to human follies, there is a nuclear war, the entire human civilisation will be wiped out. Hence, Martin Luther King was right when he said that "if we can not abolish war, war will certainly abolish us." When somebody had asked the inventor of Atom Bomb, the great scientist Einstein that which weapon we shall be fighting the 3rd World War, Einstein modestly but most poignantly replied, "I do not know about the weapon with which we shall be fighting during the 3rd World War, but I am certain that during the 4th World War, if all we have to fight, we shall be fighting with our nails and teeths. Therefore, Gandhi has most vehemently and unconditionally denounced the manufacture and use of Atom bombs (The national Gandhi museum has collected 28 statements of M. Gandhi against Atom bomb.).

Apart from the use of Atom bombs as a weapon of annihilation, the economics of Atom bomb and other traditional weapons is staggering when at least half of the human population are hungry, illiterate and without medicine. In fact, the entire economy of world development is unbalanced because of ruthless and tremendous expenditure on manufacture of war technology which is absolutely unproductive and also destructive. Therefore, Gandhi is against the manufacture of even all destructive weapons, not to speak about all wars, a world without war is certainty a Gandhian world. To Quote Him, He would not like to live in a world which is not a world of peace.

After the war, the next enemy of mankind is the concept of modern development model based on the use of most sophisticated technology based on mechanisation, automation and cybernation. Gandhi was not against machinery but against the craze for machinery. He was not an enemy of technology but he wanted a rational use of technology. In fact, technology and idéology go together. A technology without a human face is likely to generate more problems than it can solve. The report of the club of Rome and 'The Limits to Growth' has shown the limits of blind exploitation of nature. It has resulted in acid rain, the heating of the sea and the earth and the dangerous holes in the ozone layers. This has created a poisoned atmosphere and a slow but certain death of the entire human beings. Hence, the question of peace is closely related with the modern economics based on unlimited wants and unlimited exploitation of nature. At present, the USA has only 6% of the world population, but it consumes about 46% of the material resources. Such a national power necessarily requires a political control over natural resources of the world which means it must strengthen its military power to the maximum. Hence, a world economy which is based on ruthless exploitation of natural resources and blind use of mechanisation and automation are most responsible for creating atmosphere for waging wars. Hence, today, war is not only a military problem or simply a political problem but also an economic and ecological problem. We have to create economy of peace along with politics of peace for creating a peaceful world.

But the problem is how can we fight the problem of war. It can not be done only through prayers and meditations, it requires to build a new psychology, a new asceticism and a new civilisation. We must start with the limitation of our wants and create economy of permanence and peace. An economics which depends upon exploitation of man creates inequality and discontent. This is the structural cause of global unrest. Peace is not only an absence of war, it is also negation of exploitation and inequality, blind and ruthless use of natural resources and creating a politics of power and domination.

While dealing with the problem of peace, Gandhi was not an utopian but he was a practical idealist. He knew that war is the result of war politics and more of war economics. Hence, unless, a complete overhaul of our entire political and economic system are taken into considerations, peace will remain an impossibility. For this, he has emphasised the important pedagogy of peace, as was begins in the minds of men, the defences of peace can also be built in the minds of men. Unless, we change the mental set-up from the kindergarten upto the university students with the pedagogy of peace, we cannot achieve the ultimate result even in a century. Alexander Pope has rightly said, "It is education that forms the common mind, just as the twig is bent, the tree is inclined." It means to win a war against violence and war, we have to start from ABC of peace education, peace research and peace action. It may take not more than a decade to create a peaceful world because this is not a matter of utopian exercise but an urgency of supreme importance. This is a question of life and death and hence if we take up the cause of peace as a Gandhian Satyagrahi, we shall overcome all the obstacles in our way and peace will be at our doorsteps. Gandhi was a peace volunteer and also a peace commander. As a commander, he ordered for martyrdom and as a peace volunteer, he became a peace martyr. Indeed, "Blessed are the peace—makers!

10

Freedom Through Satyagraha

I

"In the golden age of Asia, Korea was one of its lamp-bearers And that lamp is waiting to be delighted again, for the illumination of the East."

There are the words from Indian Nobel Laureate R.N Tagore, who epitomized the Indian spirituality, thought, literature and art. Although politically detached, he always protested against unjustice as a matter of moral duty. He inspired the humankind to resist the forces of colonialism whether in India or Korea. Korea, then under the Japanese colonial rule looked forward to such inspirations and had invited Tagore to visit their country. Though Tagore could not visit Korea then, he was deeply moved by the invitation extended to him through Korean patriotic feelings which found expression in the poem.[1] Not only this he supported the Korean cause even in front of a crowd in Japan in 1924, notwithstanding the protocol. As the poet had led an agitation against the partition of Bengal by the then colonial powers and had surrendered his knighthood when he heard of the brutal killing of hundreds of innocent and peaceful Indians at Jallianwala Bagh in Punjab so Tagore had sympathized with the Korean non-violent mass resistance as a human being. What had been expressed on the surface, might have been like the tip of the iceberg of his deep anguish and agony and fierce anger that lay in his heart.

There is a marked similarity between Korean and Indian

struggle of Independence. Just as the Japanese ruthlessly attempted to suppress Korean nationalism whenever it appeared and thousands were killed and imprisoned; in the first years after annexation in 1910, and there were 70 separate encounters between Korean patriot-insurgents and Japanese authorities, similarly in India as early as in 1857, an armed revolt called the First War of Indian Independence was started to end the political domination and economic exploitation by the British colonialists. But unfortunately, because of multiples factors, the battle was lost. Repression and oppression reacted their climax. Then it was challenged by innumerable freedom-fighters courting life-imprisonment and facing gallows. A desire to resist oppression is implemented in the nature of man. While moderate section adopted the constitutional method of prayer, petition and delegations, the fire-brand youngmen, like the chivalorous Koreans took to insurgency, terrorism etc. to fight the colonial rule. However, when Gandhi assumed the leadership after his return from South Africa, where he had fought a crucial non-violent fight against racial discrimination under the garb of colonialism, the mainstream of Indian Freedom Movement assumed a peaceful, non-violent but powerful mass-character. The nationalism of colonial peoples that followed World War I had its impact in Korea. On March 1, 1919, a Proclamation of Korean Independence was issued by 33 Prominent Koreans. This is exactly similar to the proclamation of Complete Independence on 26th January 1930 under the leadership of Mahatama Gandhi and Jawaharlal Nehru the rough out the whole of India. Similarly, in Korea, about 50,000 people took part in peaceful demonstrations whenever the proclamation was read. According to the Japanese reports, during the movement for Independence in Korea which tasted in full vigour for two months, 533 Koreans were killed, 1409 wounded and 19054 imprisoned. The Japanese Govt. being unpopular had to recall its Governor General Yoshimichi Hasegawa and appointed Admiral Makoto Saito. However, many Korean patriots were agitating for Korean Independence outside Korea in Siberia, Manchuria, China and

U.S.A. This was similarly done during Indian freedom struggle, when many Indian patriots tried to mobilize world opinion in favcur of India's Independence. It was Gandhi's great ingenuity that he could enlist the active support of many eminent Britishers, prominent Europeans and Americans in his "battle of right against might." Again an exactly exciting similar dimension we can find in the Freedom Movements both in Korea and India, to install National Government in exile. The Korean nationalists abroad after the March Movement, set up a provisional government with Head quarters in Sanghai. This is similar to setting up *Free India.* Govt. in exile by Raja Mahendra Pratap and later by Subhas Chandra Bose in South Asia in 1946. Mr. Bose not only set up a full-fledged parallel Govt. but also set up Indian National Army which fought the Britishers in Burma and also onside Indian boarder. The Korean nationalists also continued their activities outside their country upto War II. A permanent Korean Commission was established in Washington D.C. They lose also active even in Japan and an unsuccessful attempt is as made on the life of Japanese Emperor to average the cruel repression by the Japanese rulers. In India one Indian youth avenged the brutal mass massacre of peaceful Indians at Jallianwala Bagh by killing the King pin of this sordid inhuman drama of mass-murder. However, World War II brought an end to both Japanese rule in Korea and British rule in India. A provisional government in Korea was set up in 1946, so it was in India. Due to reasons beyond their control, both Korea and India suffered the torments of partition. There was war between the South and North Korea which lasted for three years in which one million lives were lost. In India also in the wake of partition, an undeclared civil war in the form of communal riots ravaged both Pakistan and India resulting in not only the death of almost one hundred thousand people but displacement of more than 30 millions people and that has followed three boarder wars. But I am constrained to believe that these wars are the result of colonial legacy which works on Divide and Rule Policy.

II

Apart from simulanty in the strategies of Freedom Movement between Korea and India, there is deeper cultural and spiritual roots between them. If legends are to be believed, India and Korea enjoy a prehistoric relationship. During the Ist Century A.D., a Korean king named Kim-Suro of Kaya Kingdom had married a princess of *Ayodhya*, the Kingdom of the great Indian hero and incarnation Lord Ram. During the Mahabharata period, the dynasty of the *Kurus* are said to have gone upto Korea in pursuit of cultural odyssey. Coming to the more recent and the period of recorded history, Buddhism has been a strong bond between Korea and India. Buddhism is perhaps the most precious gift that the far Eastern countries received from India, which is the homeland of Buddhism. However as Korea being surrounded on three sides by the sea, Buddhism found its way to Korea as a result of the influence of China. Buddhism came to Korea as early as in the 4th century A.D. and slowly through the benevolent royal patronage of kingdoms of *Shilla, Koguryo* (328 A.D) *Paekche* (600 A.D), *Karyo* (918-1392 A.D), and through the scholarly dedication of some of Indian monks like Sundo (4th Century A.D) Maranand (384 A.D), *Mukhejha* (4th Century A.D) and Korean Bhikkhus like *Kutik* (who studied in India) that Buddhism began to be Practised by the common people and it became the life-pattern of India. Even killing of animals was regarded as a wrong act.[2] However, due to many reasons, there was decline of Buddhism. The *Yl* dynasty (1392-1910 A.D) adopted Confuscianism in 1910 with the Japanese occupation of Korea, there was an attempt to introduce into Korea Buddhist sects affiliated to Japan. But anti-Japanese mood of the Koreans did not welcome it. Today one third of population in Korea are Buddhists. There are 7244 Buddhist temples, 22200 Bhikkhus and even some full fledged Buddhist Universities.

III

Although the golden days of Buddhism both in Korea and India have become mostly the glories of the past, we cannot deny that there is still strong impact of Buddhistic ideals on life-pattern including the Freedom Movement of both countries. Gandhi has inherited the Buddhist legacy of compassion and non-violence, which signifies a state of complete peace and harmony in the life of the individual as well as the society as a whole. In the Buddhist tradition, the penacle is reached in the spiritual state of *Brahma Vihara,* which implies the inculcation, nourishing and development of the four-fold sublime states-friendliness (*metta*), compassion (*Karuna*), loving kindness (*mudita*) and equanimity (*upekha*)[3]. Of the five precepts (*Panch-Shila*), of Buddhism, "abstination from taking life" of others is the first one. The very idea of "the well-being of all" (*Sabbe Satta Bhavantu Sukhitatta*)[4] also positively suggests the idea of non-violence (*Ahimsa*). Hence, non-violence is the most important concept of Buddhist tradition. But it does not mean a weapon of the weak and surrender to injustice. Buddha fearlessly carried the war into the enemy's camp and brought down on its knees an arrogant priesthood. But even as Buddha indulged in intense direct action, he showed unmistakable love and gentleness behinds his action. Hence, he is no follower of Buddha, who being afraid to die, takes flight before any danger, all the while wishing that somebody else would remove the danger by destroying the person causing it.

To Gandhi, "non-violence is a universal principle and its operation is not limited by a hostile environment. Indeed its efficacy can be tested only when it acts in the midst of and in spite of opposition." [4A CH 30.6.36.] Our non-violence would be hollow thing and nothing worth, if it depended for its success on the goodwill of the authorities. Like a practical idealist, to Gandhi, "truth and non-violence are no cloistered virtues but applicable as much in the forum and the legislatives as in the market place." [4B (H 8.5.37)] So Gandhi did not agree with those that truth and non-violence have no place in politics or freedom struggle. He had no use for truth and non-violence as or means of individual salvation. Their application in everyday life had been his life-long experiment. *Secondly,* he did not like truth and non-violence to remain for mere individual practice but for practice by groups and communities and nations. Non-violence is attribute of the soul, and therefore, to be practiced by everybody in all affairs of life.

Freedom is everybody's birth right. But "it can never be a free gift by one nation to another. It is a treasure to be purchased with a nation's best blood"[5] There is no such thing as slow freedom. Freedom is like a birth. Till we are fully free, we are slaves. All birth takes place in a moment.[6] Gandhi knew the price of freedom. He said : "In our march towards true freedom, we must be prepared for repetitions of the wrong such as Jallianwala Bagh massacre." [7] He was convinced that "no country has ever risen without being purified through the force of suffering. The other suffers so that her child may live. The condition of wheat growing is that the seed grain should perish."[8] He further exhorts : "That nation is great which rests its head upon death as its pillow."[9] "A nation that is capable of limitless sacrifice is capable of rising to limitless heights."[10]

But in his fearlessness, he did not see the exchange of British brute force for any other brute force. He contended that the revolutionary method of violence cannot succeed in India. He wrote his master-key book *Hind Swaraj* or *Indian Home Rule* (1908) in answer to the Indian school of violence. He had come into contact with every known anarchist in London. Their bravery impressed him but he felt that their zeal was misguided. But he felt that violence was no remedy for India's ills, and that her civilization required the use of a different higher weapon for self-protection. "The world is weary of hate. We see the fatigue overcoming the Western nations. We see that this song of hate has not benefitted humanity. Let it be the privilege of India to turn a new leaf and act a lesson to the world."[11] One might of course say that there can be no non-violent rebellion and there has been none known to history. It was Gandhi's ambition to provide an instance, and it was his dream that his country may win its freedom through non-violence. I would like to repeat to the world times without number, and he will not purchase my country's freedom at the cost of non-violence. Gandhi had many reasons to discard violence as method of achieving freedom. "Science of war leads one to dictatorship pure and simple. Science of non-violence alone can lead one to pure democracy."[12] However, for argument sake, if we presume that India produced sufficient arms and ammunition and men who knew the art of war, it can be replied that in a non-violent war even women and children would contribute an equal share with physically the strongest. His resistance to war does not carry me to the point of thwarting those who wish to take part in it but Gandhi reasoned with them. He put before them the better way and leave them to make the choice. According to him it is beneath the dignity of men to resort to mutual slaughter. He could afford to look at the butchery going on in the world with indifference. People might well applaud whole-heartedly the action of Mustafa Kamal Pasha, De Valera and Lenin. But India was not like Turkey or Ireland or Russia. His accumulated experience of more than fifty years in South Africa and India filled him with the greatest hopes that in the adoption of non-violence lies the future of India and the world. In fact, Gandhi had to chose between allying himself to violence or finding out some other method of meeting the crisis. "Thus came into being the moral equivalent of war."[13] He distinguished between evil and evil-does. He must not harbour ill-will or bitterness against the latter. Hence, his motto of life was to try to overcome evil by good, anger by love, untruth by truth, *himsa* by *ahimsa*.[14] Gandhi held himself to be incapable of hating any being on earth. Hate is the subtlest form of violence. We cannot be really non-violent and yet have hate in us."[15] It seems that Gandhi is Buddha born again. Lord Buddha says : "From anger, anger is not satiated". There is no fin like passion (*Raga*), no losing through like hatred, there is no pain like this body, there is no happiness higher than rest."[16] We should also remember that the modern State has become more powerful than Leviathan, because of progress in science and technology. Hence, it is more difficult to face the modern

State with sporadic violence or terrorism. Besides, violence leads to counter-violence which never ends, often it leads to civil war as we find in Bosnia, Afghanistan, Burma, Kampuchea etc. Even recent history is a witness that a violent revolution in France has led to the emergence of a dictator like Nepolean, in England, murder of Charles I, brought Cromwell and in Russia the Czar was replaced by Stalin. It means that a violent struggle endangers democratic fibre besides creating a climate of suspicion, hatred, revenge and violence, as they are the result of hopes long-deferred and aspirations ruthlessly suppressed.[17] In violent struggle even the legitimate participation is not possible. If we depend upon the barrel of the gun for the vindication of our cause, then one who can yield greater violence may claim that justice lies in his side. A revolution cannot be identified with violence otherwise even acts of murder or every bloody war however unjust they might be called revolution. "Violence may destroy one or more bad rulers, but like Ravana's head, others will pop up in their places.[18]

Gandhi's mission was more than achieving India's Independence. He endeavoured to show to his countrymen that "violent non-cooperation only multiplies evil"[19] and "the religion of non-violence is not meant merely for the *rishis* and saints. It is meant for common people as well. Non-violence is the law of our species as violence is the law of the brute...The dignity of man requires obedience to a higher law—to the strength of the spirit...The *rishis* (seers), who discovered the law of non-violence in the midst of violence, were greater geniuses than Newton. They were themselves greater warriers than Wellington. Having themselves known the use of arms, they realized their uselessness and taught a weary world that its salvation lay not through violence but through non-violence."[20] It was Gandhi's ambition and dream that this country win its freedom through non-violence. And as he said he "would like to repeat to the world times without number that I will not purchase my country's freedom at the cost of non-violence." My marriage to non-violence is such an absolute thing that I would rather commit suicide than he deflected from my position.[21] True democracy can never come through untruthful and violent means. Individual freedom can have the fullest play only under a regime of unadulterated *ahimsa*.[22] In its positive form, non-violence means the largest love, the greatest charity. "Having flung aside the sword, there is nothing except the cup of love which I can offer to those who oppose me"[23]—he said He could not think of a permanent enemity between man and man. Love is the strongest force the world possesses. "The hardest heart and the grossest ignorance must disappear before the rising sun of suffering without anger and without malice."[24] His goal was friendship with the whole world and "he could combine the greatest love with the greatest opposition to wrong."[25] However, Gandhi's non-violence was "not merely a passive spirituality that spends itself in idle meditation, but it will be an active thing which will carry war into the enemy's camp.[26] Non-violence presupposes ability to strike. It has no room either for cowardice, or vegenence. There is hope for a violent man to be some day non-violent and cowardice go ill together. Similarly vegenence too is a weakness, which comes out of tear of harm. But non-violence is impossible without fearlessness. Hence he said : "where there is choice between cowardice and violence, I would advice violence."[27] "I would risk violence a thousand times than the emasculation of a whole race."[28] But there are limitations of violence. It is intended to exert pressure, but it is the insane pressure of anger and ill-will, while non-violent acts exert pressure far more effective than violent act, for that pressure comes from goodwill and gentleness. It works subtly and invisibly, the surest and quickest way.

Conclusion : It is believed that there can be no non-violent rebellion and there has been none known to history. Korean and Indian freedom struggle have of the recent past have atleast partially refuted this belief. Perhaps, both Korea and India have the common legacy of spirituality and compassion of Buddha. Apart from Lord Buddha, India has a continuing tradition of non-violence from the ancient Vedas upto Gandhi. Non-violence is regarded as the supreme virtue. However, it was Gandhi who brought non-violence from the high pedestal of individual virtue to the religion of the common men. It is a universal principle applicable as much in the forum and the legislatures as in the market place. It has place in politics and worldly affairs. Then it is not matters for mere individual practice but for social action also. Gandhi has demonstrated the efficacy of non-violent massive mass-action during Indian Freedom Struggle. He adopted the double dynamics of *agitational method (Satyagraha)*, (Strike, Demonstration, Boycott, Non-cooperation, Civil Disobedience, Fasting including Fast Unto Death) and *Constructive Programme* (like Communal Harmony, Eradication of Indian Apartheid, Prohibition, Rural Industries, Basic Education, National Language, Service to Women, Tribal People, etc.). Constructive Programme is the construction of complete Independence. Non-violent direct action is and aid to Constructive programme and is a full substitute for armed revolt. In fact the goal of Constructive Programme is the achievement of Independence and it is achieved in the measure Constructive programme is fulfilled.

Non-violent resistance is as old as resistance through violence. There has been examples of Socrates, Jesus and others. Gandhi tried to practice it on collective level. So we find in Korea in 1910 after Japanese occupation. But there are a few more instances of non-violent mass resistance. During mid 19th Century (1860-67), when Emperor Frnz Josef's attempts to subjugate Hungry to the Austrian power and moderates felt helpless, a Catholic landowner Ferene Deak not only protested but also organised independent Hungarian education, agriculture and industry, and boycott of Jails, Parliament. There was also non-violent resistance against military action and finally Emperor had to give Hungry her constitution. The struggle against social and racial discrimination in South Africa was started in 1906 and there were appreciable achievements. In India, apart from National Struggle for Independence in 1921-22 (Non-cooperation), Civil

Disobedience (1929-30), Individual Satyagraha (1940), and Quit India Movement (1942), there were successful non-violent mass action in Champaran (1917), Vykom (1925), Kotagarh (1921), Bardoli (1928), Ahmedabad (1917), Kheda (1926-27), Borsad (1923), Nagpur (1927), Salt Satyagraha (1930) were organized. In Denmark, in 1940 without previous preparation, training in non-violent resistance, Danish people organized defiance against ruthless Nazis. In Norway again in 1940, non-violent Resistance was organized in which youth in athletic clubs, Judges of the Supreme Court etc. participation. Education on Nazi pattern was boycotted. We know about non-violent resistance against segregation laws in U.S.A. in 1955 under the leadership of Martin Luther King. In modern Poland, the Polish people started a non-violent mass action under Walesa against the Communist martial regime and they succeeded. Even in 1st World War coal miners of the Rhur in Germany non-violent resistance was organized. In Gold Coast, after 10 years of non-violent resistance, Nkrumah was freedom. Recently, in U.S.S.R., it was non-violent mass action that had compelled the military leaders to free Gorachev. Even in Japan, under Rev. Fuji Guruji, successful non-violent action was organized to stop Tokyo airport for nuclear base. In India during 1975-76, when civil right were traupled, a massive non-violent mass movement arose in which the then ruler and her party was thrown into the dustbin of history.

Violence has lost its dynamics. If we want a world without war, we also should have a struggle for national independence without violence, terrorism. If we allow terrorism and violence, we cannot hope to banish nuclear war. Hence, either we have non-violent resistance or non-existence of the entire humanity.

REFERENCES

1. Poem by R.N. Tagore, Bengali translation by Deepak Roy 'Pracher Deep'.
2. *Encycleopaedia Britannica.*
3. Ghosh, I.M., *Ahimsa-Buddhism and Gandhian,* Delhi : Indian

Bibliographies Bureau, 1988, Preface, V.

4. *Ibid.*, p. 59. See *Dhammapada*, Verse 270 (ed. S. Radhakrishnan) Oxford University Press, 1950.
5. Gandhi, M.K., *Young India*, 5.1.1922.
6. *Ibid.*, 9.3.1922.
7. *Ibid.*, 18.2.1920.
8. *Ibid.*, 16.6.1920.
9. Gandhi, M.K., *Hind Swaraj* or *Indian Home Rule*, Ahmedabad, Navjivan Publishing House, 1944, p. 48.
10. Gandhi, M.K., *Young India*, 25.8.1920.
11. Gandhi, M.K., Gandhi in Indian Village, by M. Desai, Madras : S. Ganesan, 1927, p. 166.
12. Gandhi, M.K., *Harijan*, 15.10.1938.
13. *Ibid.*, *Young India*, 5.11.1931.
14. *Ibid.*, 8.8.1929.
15. *Ibid.*, 17.8.1934.
16. *Dhammapada*, 251 (Mala Vaggo).
17. Young, K., *Social Psychology*, London : Kegan Paul, p. 439.
18. Gandhi, M.K., *Harijan*, 21.9.1934.
19. *Ibid.*, *Young India*, 23.3.1922.
20. *Ibid.*, 11.8.1920.
21. *Ibid.*, 12.11.1931.
22. Gandhi, M.K., *Harijan*, 27.5.1939.
23. *Ibid.*, *Young India*, 2.4.1931.
24. *Ibid.*, 29.2.1925.
25. *Ibid.*, 10.3.1920.
26. *Ibid.*, 12.5.1920.
27. *Ibid.*, 11.8.1920.
28. *Ibid.*, *Harijan*, 20.7.1935.

11

Satyagraha : As a Moral Equivalent of Terrorism and Violence

Violence in the 21st century has become so dreadful that it can wipe out not only our civilization and culture but also our existence. No doubt, there is an element of violence inherent in human nature and therefore we have fought with each other with nails and teeth. But later on we invented new weapons of war as stools. During Paleolithic and Neolithic ages we fought with crude stones and pointed stones. Next in the evolutionary framework we invented sticks, arrows and clubs for fighting. In the metallic age we invented spears, swords and many weapons for fighting made of steel and brass. During the gun powder age we had guns, machine guns and bombs for war operations. However, in the 20th and 21st centuries we have atomic weapons. According to rough but reliable estimate there are at present about 40 thousand nuclear weapons which are deadlier than those used at Hiroshima and Nagasaki. If there is an atomic war it can wipe out entire human civilization at least seven times with the atomic arsenals reserved at different places. Though the U.S.A. and some western powers and China have the monopoly of atomic weapons but according to reports forty seven countries have some excess to atomic power. At present though there is only occasional full fledged wars as in Korea, Vietnam, Kampuchia, Iraq, Afghanistan and the middle east countries etc., we have the greatest threat from growing amount of terrorism all over the world whether it is U.S.A. 7/11 or U.K. blasts or India or Pakistan etc. There is every likelihood that through purchase or theft or some other form of help the terrorists may acquire atomic bombs and weapons sooner than later. It is clear they have no international legal binding or moral sense of human safety and they can use these weapons indiscriminately when they are in their hands. It is beyond the control of super powers to control the situation and bring scur to humanity.

Hence either we search out a moral equivalent of war or we prepared for being wiped out of our existence. But what would be the moral equivalent, will it be unabashed and totally illegal invasion on smaller countries by super powers either on Iraq by U.S.A. or on Vietnam by People's Republic of China or anywhere else. So if war is out of question can narrow nationalism or the concept of personal religion come to our rescue. In the name of narrow nationalism we have fought out six thousand five hundred big and small wars in human history and similarly we have about 7 thousand bloody wars fought in the name of religion. Even in the same religion of Christianity the Catholics and Protestants fought for hundred years of war. So also the different sects of Hindus, Muslims etc. have worse records of hatred and violence in the name of religion.

Hence unless we try to discover a substitute for "nationalism" and "personal religion", we cannot save our human existence. Now taking the concept of narrow nationalism we have the concept of world government as a feeling moral substitute. Starting from Socrates and the Vedas and upto Wendel Wilkie 'One World', H.G. Wales, Pt. Rahul his novel 'On 22nd Century. We have been given some hints as Etopia. But one world government is neither an ethopia nor a dreaming paradise. But a hard choice and the only alternative for modern times. We have only one choice either we choose atom or one world. Secondly, we have to reconsider our attitude towards personal and sectarian religions. I do not reject the various contributions of religions professing moral and spiritual virtues. But at present they have become out of date. There has been a virtual clash of civilization "Hutcheson" in the name of personal religions. The middle east, the Kashmir region and the European and African countries have also experienced the bloody hatricidal wars in the name of religion. Hence either we develop a universal religion based on pure morality and spirituality or brush aside religious dogmas enciting violence as the opium of the people.

Next to the outdated concept of nationalism and personal religions we have a new challenge in the face and exploitative concept of so called liberalization, privatization and globalization which is perhaps the greatest threat to world peace and harmony.

In the name of so called Globalization, the I.M.F., the World Bank and the W.T.O. have been creating two worlds—a world of haves and a world of have-nots. There has been subtle attempt to impose new imperialism in the grab of economic reforms. In the recent wealth report of the U.N.O. it is clearly said that the wealth has no doubt increased but it lies only in the hands of a small minority. For example in India only 15% people have become wealthy and rich but the condition of 85% is wretched and poor. Hence with the growth of wealth there has been growth of inequality. This is the state of all over the world in the Third World countries. Hence we have to evolve a new global economic structure based on non-exploitation and equality.

As a foot note on the concept of Satyagraha may I venture to suggest that we need a non-violent war against unjust socio-economic and political structure of our society. Since violence is out of date, self-suicidal and anti-civilization non-violence is the only alternative. Not to bring the theoretical justification for Satyagraha or psychological arguments put forward by Richard Gray in his book 'The Power of Non-violence' and by Lek Velissa etc. I will like the people to consider the miracle of Satyagraha in modern times. Without dwelling upon the martyrdom of Socrates in Greece, of beheading martyrdom of Mansoor, crucification of Jesus Christ and recent martyrdom of Mahatma Gandhi, Lincoln and Martin Luther King. The Indian sub-continent has broken the chains of slavery through non-violence under the then first rate world power of the world. Even with recent past Martin Luther King won the battle of racial equality in the U.S.A. without weapon of violence. Violence is not only unpractical but it is counter-productive. Violence has brought worst peril in human history and has substituted tyranny and despots with the established weak power.

In France Napolean came after violent revolution during Louis fourteenth. Crownwell rose as a dictator after killing Charles 1st and Stalin seized the power and became a dictator after killing the Czars. Along our neighbourhood Pakistan, Bangladesh, Thailand and Burma have lost their democratic structure because in the name of violent reforms the dictators have always the upper hand. Hence Satyagraha as the path of truth and non-violence has the ingredients of fighting structural violence as well as creating a world of love and peace.

It is apparent that as war has lost its dynamics in this atomic age. Similarly social change through violence has been becoming gradually out of date and unproductive. Hence it is imperative to search an equivalence of change without violence. Satyagraha offers such an alternative which rejects both violence as well as structural injustices of all kinds. If blood shed is violence social and economic injustice are also violence perhaps more deadlier than over-violence. Hence we need a world without war and society without violence of all kinds. But one can argue that the religious saints and sears have been singing the music of love and non-violence from time immemorial. But violence has not been abolished. There is no doubt about the pure intentions of the saints and sages about their prophecy of love and non-violence. But perhaps they thought that if there is love and non-violence in the hearts of man there will also be reflections of love in social and economic affairs. But history has showed that the vested interests in religion have outweighed the simple and pure intensions of the saints and many forms of exploitations and discrimination including human cruelty have clouded impurity of religion.

Hence we have to free religion from dogmatism and unnecessary ritualism. In fact only then religion can be acceptable. This brings to us the glimpse of inner spirituality which should be combined with scientific outlook. Satyagraha as a weapon of social change is a science of triple transformation—change of heart, change of ideas and the change of circumstances. This is a task for social sciences to invent a dynomatics of both change of hearts and ideas. Change of heart is no fiction of imagination but it is a reality. It is a psychological truth that there has been real conversion of man from forsaking its evil habits and adopting better mode of behaviour. We have to frame a scientific calculus for change of heart on an individual and on mass level. But changes of heart has to be supplemented in this age of knowledge and science. We find large scale propaganda for both political and ideological changes. Even religion have taken this path of propaganda and the help of several trans media. Even the religious and political extremists have been using this instrument of ideological propaganda and brain-washing to train their cadres to adopt violence. Violence even to this extent of human bombing. Hence if we can develop ideological changes through logies and reason, we can achieve a lot of success. The change of circumstances is in favour of Satyagraha method of war and change. This is more appropriate, effective and humane.

12

Structural and Institutional Dimensions of Global Peace

The traditional approach as early as Socrates who had said—"I am neither an athenian nor a Greek, but a citizen of world." In the same spirit, the Vedas had proclaimed through a Prayer "I am the progeny of the Mother Earth". Similarly almost all religions, the doctrine of the Father or God and the Brotherhood of man has been acclaimed as the supreme commandment. The prayer in the holy Quran clearly says that God is the preserver and the guardian of the entire creation; Almin—Al Fhatiah! But it is a tragedy that the Religion which literally means "to bind together" has been a source of millions of massacres, oppression and exploitation, bigotory and orthodoxy. According to reliable testimony nearly six thousand five hundred small and big wars have been fought in the name of religions in the human history. Islam had its Jehad and the Christianity called it crusades and fight of hundred years of war between two sects of same Christianity. True religions have fought for the mankind to move from savagery to civilization, from cannibalism to vegetarianism, from arsan and anarchy and from hatred and violence to love and peace, but it is also a stark reality that it has also engineered narrowness, rivalry and even different kinds of oppressive discrimination based on superstitions of birth, gender and many artificial cobwebs. This traditional and research approach have been given nearing five thousand years of experimentations in achieving peace making but it has not been able to achieve success. Religion and politics have become two sides of the same phenomena for dividing humanity power with the resulting that both kingship and the peperi and the paple supreme have fought a grievous battle of which the Vatican is the cast vestiage of the theocratic power with the secular might of the political power.

Hence peace has become a distant dream. Apart from the traditional religious approach for global peace, we have also efforts of humanitarians and pacifists to establish peace in the world. But because of some fundamental structural and institutional approach the efforts of these well intensioned persons have not brought relief to the mankind.

Structural Peace

War begins in the minds of man, therefore the defences of peace can be built in the minds of man. But this dictum of UINESCO has been regarded more as a religious sermon rather than a programme of action. In fact, violence is ingrained in our societal structure. To start with economic life, one third of the globe have been enjoying comforts and luxuries while the rest of humanity mostly in Asia and Africa have been ruling under grim poverty, unemployment and inequality. It seems the world is divided between the rich and the poor, developed and developing. Even now either the world body like the U.N.O. have not been able to bridge the great gulf between the have's and the have not's. Earlier capitalist system had mercilessly exploited the raw materials and minerals through imperialistic system based on military force. At present new imperialism has taken its place in the name of liberalism, privatization and globalization. We have an exploitative economic structure which breeds violence and thwarts efforts for global peace. If war for blood shed is violence, exploitation, inequality and profiteering are also uglier forms of violence. We cannot have global peace if we have such an unfavourable economic structures. Recent examples of invasion of Iraq and Afghanistan and Ugoslavia and threat over Iran, Pakistan and North Korea etc. are invincible proofs of economic causes of war.

Political Structure

Economic system and economic interests influence our political system, whereas political system also influence our economic structure. Hence they go hand in hand. Politics has ceased to be a science of brotherhood. It has become a more machiavellian than dealt in the famous fretory. 'The Prince' Our political system is based on deceit and dishonesty, falsity, fraud, exploitation and bossism. Hence it is bound to usher violence in the world. Perhaps with grab of nationalism modern political state has usurped the power of the people and has become more autocratic and dictatorial even the sacred cow of narrow nationalism has been the most potent cause of violence in the world. The 20th century has been a century of nationalism. Following the foot steps of Julius Caesar and Alexander the Great, Hitler in the modern time wanted to be a world conqueror through savage war. Even now the great powers specially U.S.A. has been behaving as a world policeman. In the case of Iraq and other places it seems that our political system based on sovenistic nationalism has become outdated. For world peace we urgently need a world governance and a world polity based on equality and non-exploitation. Tolstoy and Gandhi had rightly advocated purification of politics because true politics is brotherhood which is a branch of ethics. Gandhi therefore advocated spiritualization of politics. But today there is not only politics for power and self interest but it is also a cult of criminalization. From much centralization breeds violence whether it is in politics or economics. Hence a world government will be a decentralized federal Govt. of different states enjoying utmost freedom and equality. World peace is impossible with the existence of either military pacts like NATO or Atlantic nor it is possible with super powers like G-8 or G-4.

Cultural Structure

Like economics and politics our educational and cultural systems are also rooted in violence. We need a world where the mind is free and the head is high. At present our educational system is based on the spirit of competition which legacy of the Darvinian systems of struggle for existence and survival of the fittest. Any educational system based on the cult of competition cannot create a society of peace and harmony and man can not and should not have competition with another man because it only create an atmosphere of hatred, jealousy and envy. Therefore the entire educational system should be based on co-operation and non-violence aid rather than co-operation of one man with other.

To treat one's religion as the most conducive for the development of human progress and the rest others in the clutches of the devils is perverted absolutalism and degenerated intellectual violence. Hence the only way out to treat all religions with equal respects and evolve a kind of universal religion which will be the real religion of man.

Social Violence in Social Structure

Though the mankind is one and undivided and the human race is one and only one but our folly have led us to divide ourselves on the basis of race and religion, birth and colour, nationality and gender etc. If humanity is one any attempt for such distinction is anti-man and anti-civilization.

Institutional Dimension of Peace

India has achieved perhaps the greatest height in the field of spiritual engineering but it is not so in the realm of social engineering and organizational engineering. At the level of the world we have to create such institutions or organizations which can further cause of global peace. During the last century we had hundreds of smaller and big conflicts. One, deadlier than the other. Besides, there have been two world wars and we are on the brink of the third world war which will mean total annihilation of human species. Hence the League of Nations and the UNO have not been able to fulfil the aspirations of the mankind for abolishing the fear of war. Even now almost every state of the world have smaller and bigger armies and modern weapons of destination. Nearly it is a sad commentary for educational world to carry on education of war and military science instead of teaching military science to the young generation. We should enforce syllabi in peace education, conflict resolution and peace research. Alexander Pope said—It is education that forms the common mind.

Just as the twig is bent, the tree is inclined. In short, peace education is the foundation for a peaceful world. Education is also a very important component of our culture because it not only moulds our mind and trains our intellect. It goes to create a new frame of personality for a new world. Like education we have accepted the dynamics of competition as the only efficient method for progress in our cultural life and therefore we have adopted competition in the field of sports, music, dance and drama etc. In short, our whole cultural system is based on competition which breeds psychological and intellectual violence.

In the field of religion the concept of personal religion have become outdated. Every religious sect regards its own religion, the oldest and best.

20 billion dollars are being spent over the military and its hardware. There are about a dozen countries having nuclear weapons in their possessions but the UNO has become a tool of consolidating the vested interests of a few super powers. Hence it is imperative to create institutions of peace and harmony in the world. We have to set up a UNO of peace and instead of sending a cadre of peace army (Shanti Sena). Similarly we have to establish universities or institutes of these all over the world in good number.

In short, global peace needs a new civilization and a new culture. Unless we are able to attack structural violence peace will remain a day dream. Similarly instead of establishing temples, mosques, churches etc. of different religions we should set up temple of peace and harmony everywhere. The most optimistic note about global peace is based on the logic that violence has lost its dynamics. War has become out of date because world war with atomic weapons will leave none alive. Both sides will be completely annihilated in an atomic war. Hence there is no choice and the peace is only alternative. Similarly for eliminating violence in society violence has become productive because it leads either to fundamentalism and extremism or it leads to dictatorship. Hence we have to develop moral equivalence of violence even for social and political change. We must not tolerate social and economic inequality but we should also not take the help of violence which is self defeating. Gandhi, mutual can be revised through non-violence that is Satyagraha. Satyagraha therefore is a positive instrument to fight structural violence and institutional violence.

13

Strategies and Stratagems in Satyagraha

It is most welcome to share my ideas in an intellectual enterprise to examine the status of Gandhian Strategies in this century-year of writing Hind Swaraj which is an undisputable manifesto of Gandhian ideology. At the outset, I may submit that Gandhian thought is an open an ever-evolving system based on practical experience. But it is important to note that Gandhian Strategies can not be considered at the cost of Gandhian fundamental postulates of *truth* and non-*violence*. Even his truth and non-violence are not absolute and static concepts. Hence, Gandhi does not prefer to be a bonded-slave of so called 'consistency'. To him, such an undynamic concept of truth is not his ideal. Therefore, he grew from truth to truth and also his concept of non-violence had been growing and progressing. But this does not mean that he had ever sacrificed is principle for opportunistic gains. As a matter of fact, he was always ready for compromises but never at the cost of cause. Hence he adopted only those strategies which were in conformity with his fundamental principles. The Eleven Vows' were his basic moral postulates and '18 Point Constructive Programmes' were his practical guide lines determining his strategies. Even in matters of Satyagraha the basic principles of truths and non violence determined all his actions and his strategies. This means that there is an integral and intimate relationship between ends and means.

Ends and Means

So instead of cleverness or cunningness, he stuck steadfast to honesty, sincerity and humility. Unlike Machiavellian politics, he believed and practiced 'Spiritualisation of politics' or 'Goodness Politics'. Without moral and spiritual basis, politics has become a refuge of the scoundrels. Hence, they adopted political strategies based on falsity and fraud, deceit and dishonestly violence and bloodshed.

The questions of purity of means cannot be properly conceived without understanding the nature of man.

Nature of Man

If we think that man is nasty, brutish and selfish, we cannot think of any reform of human society. If man is regarded essentially as evil in nature it is an insult to entire humanity. Besides this is a gospel of utter pessimism. History of mankind is a record of its march from violence to non-violence from cannibalism to animal protection. No doubt we started our conflicts with fellow beings with our nails and teeth, then we quarrelled with each other with stones in Paleolithic and Neolithic Ages, with bamboo sticks, arrows etc. Later on with sword, spear etc., in metal age, with guns, machine guns and bombs of different verities during gun powder stage and now with atomic arsenals in this atomic age. Now we cannot move further. We have come to a dead end. It seems that war has lost its dynamics.

Dynamics of Non-violence

The USA with 30 thousands nuclear warheads could not use them during Vietnam war in spite of the fact that fifty five thousand precious American Soldiers were killed. USA could not use atomic weapons even in Afghanistan, Iraq and Yugoslav wars. Even the Marxist minds adhering to the principle of inevitability of war have revised their doctrine and have accepted the doctrine of coexistence for world politics. Even in matters of social change violence is becoming outdated. In France when Louise XIV was killed, the reins of governmental and administration did not came to the people. But it was taken over by a dictator called Napoleon. In England, the spineless monarch Charles 1st was slaughtered, but the power did not go to the people and was taken over by another dictator Cromwell. In Soviet Russia Czar was murdered with all his family members, but then power went to the most powerful dictator of modern human history, Josheph Stalin. In our neighbourhood the father of Bangladesh with many of his family members was brutally killed in a violent coup. But the power went to the military dictators. It means that "the more of violence, the less of revolution." At the international plane we have to choose between Atom & Ahimsa, non-existence and existence. In matters of social change we have to discover a moral equivalent of violence. Here we have to choose between blood-bath-cum-dictatorship and Satyagraha. If revolution means change of our idea & ideals, values & philosophy of life. Violence will be counter productive, because we can not change any body's value of life with physical force.

Ecological Challenges and Gandhian Strategies of Life

The 21st century is facing great threat to entire human existence not so much because of terrorism and impending wars but more because of dangerous environmental pollution, acid rains, growing holes in the Ozone layers, rape of the earth, heating of earth, rising of water level in seas and change of seasons etc. The diagnosis is simple. "Nature has enough to meet our needs, but not our greed." If we cannot put limitation to our growing wants we shall be constrained to exploit nature and natural resources in the most cruel manner with the result. There is bound to be disastrous effects in environment. Unless we change our style of life and accept voluntary limitation of our wants we cannot avoid the ecological deluge. Hence Gandhian strategies of simple living and high thinking is not a religious fad or a sermon on the mount from ivory tower, but a necessity for our life.

Gandhian Strategies of Culture

According to Toffler power, wealth and knowledge are the three important features of modern civilization, but modern civilization is facing a paradox. If we move blindly in pursuit of power, wealth and knowledge without any moral and spiritual safeguards, we are likely to face a Dooms day. Hence Arnold Toynbee after examining about 30 cultures of human history has come to the conclusion that moral and spiritual elements have the greatest survival value for any civilization. Gandhi also from his common sense perception of human history has come to the conclusion, that those civilizations which had serious lack of moral and spiritual ingradients have faded away. He cites the example of ancient civilization of Sodom and Gomarah which have been wiped out of their existence because they lacked moral values and moral life. The ultimate goal of life is happiness. But whereas wealth, power and knowledge have been increasing, human happiness has been miserably decreasing. Therefore a Noble Laureate Alexis Carrel has observed that we must find out 'Science of Man ' which can give him happiness and peace of mind.

Synthesis of Science and Spirituality

When people saw Gandhi playing his spinning wheel, living in a small room of a thatched cottage and wearing a loin cloth and working with kerosene lamp, generally called him ascetic, mediaeval, anti-science and anti-progress. But Gandhi is not only the spinning wheel or living half clad life, but also a man leading a relentless war against racial discrimination in South Africa, untouchability in India, Satyagraha for the poor farmers in Champaran', Kheda, Bardoli in India and fighting British imperialism without any hatred or sense of enmity with the British people. His message was to fight with the evil not with the evil-doers.

In short, Gandhi combined science with spirituality, politics with morality and fight without hatred. Science without spirituality is blind and a curse for humanity. But spirituality and religion without rationality and scientific temper lead to religious fundamentalism, lifeless ritualism and in human social and cultural practices.

Conclusion

Gandhi was not a system builder like Kant or Hegal, Shankar or Ramanuj, but he was never a one-sided arm chair thinker. To him, life is not a water-tight compartment, which can be divided into political social, economic departments. It is an integral whole. But the most important question is : What should be the fundamental basis of human life and society? Here Gandhi discovered the twin principle of truth and non-violence. Which have been tested as pure gold during the long force of human history. Hence any consideration about the exclusion and inclusion in Gandhian Strategies must take into account the basic tenets of Gandhian thought. This does not mean that we should not try to discover new Strategies and brush aside those which have been become lifeless and obsolete. But we must be careful that the yardstick of human progress and true civilization is not contained in plentiful extravagant living at the cost of grim poverty and inequality throughout the world. To my mind Satyagraha is the best contribution of Gandhiji for the 21st century and beyond. But Satyagraha is not something new, it is as old as Prahalada and Dhruva in India and Socrates and Jesus outside. Even in presents day, we have examples of Martin Luther King, Fuji Guruji, Sol-zens-tein and many others. But they were mostly limited to the individual levels. Gandhi tried to convert the individual to the mass level of non-violent action. Satyagraha has become a science. Hence it has universal application. It can be applied in all aspects of human life—social, political, economic etc. In the matter of Peace-Science, there has been great progress in the field of conflicts-resolution in the west. There are about seventeen hundreds Peace-Science and Peace-Research Institutes in different parts of the world but mostly in the west. This is a new strategies of Satyagraha. In India, a part from various experiments made by Mahatama Gandhi, Gaffar Khan and others in the life-time of Gandhi. We have new ideas in post-Gandhian era. Doctor R.M. Lohia introduce

"Gherao " But this has not found universal acceptance as there is an element of coercion in it which is a form of material violence. Gandhi's spiritual disciple Vinoba Bhave has however tried to argue a case for subtle, subtler and subtlest form of Satyagraha to meet the horrid nature of violence. It has not been experimented on a mass level as yet. However another tallest Gandhian Jaya Prakash Narayan has demonstrated a successful mass non-violent action against temporary dictatorship and curtailment of human-rights during 74—77. There have been isolated experiments both in India and abroad in Satyagraha. Therefore, during the Satyagraha Centenary International Seminar held last year in Delhi the great octogenarian Polish leader Leh Walesa and the African leader J.M. Kunda had expressed themselves in favour of the relevance of Satyagraha in modern times. Last but not the least, Nelson Mandela had also supported the idea of Satyagraha as the only way-out for it peaceful social change in this nuclear age, in his memorable message. The Power of Satyagraha is the power of non-violence and we have to make a choice between non-violence and non-existence.

14

Statics of War and Dynamics of Peace

To say that war begins in the minds of men is an incomplete statement because mind or mental activity does not take place in isolation, human thought is the result of certain situation and circumstances. Therefore when we look at the genesis of war in the most primitive period, where there was plenty of materials for consumption and less of population, there was hardly any conflict but as our necessities began to grow there were occasional conflict and warfare. In the beginning, the human being tried to score their supremacy through manipulating physical strength and wrestling. Later on man being a tool making animal, invented tools of stones to fight against each other. During the Paleolithic age they fought with simple stone weapons. While in the Neolithic age which proved deadlier and dangerous than the previous ones. They invented weapons of war in the form of bamboo sticks and arrow. During the metal age they invented swords and spears as metallic weapons of war and in the gunpowder age, we developed guns, machineguns, bombs and other arsenals of war. However in the twentieth century, we developed atom bombs of different varieties. Now the question is whether mankind can go beyond nuclear weapons. The simple answer in no. This means that war has lost its dynamics because an atomic war would mean total annihilation of mankind and utter destruction of human civilization. Therefore either we can invent a moral and civilized equivalent of war or we should be prepared for the doomsday.

Isn't it startling that the strongest nuclear powers like

the U.S.A. or U.S.S.R. (Russia), U.K., France and China could not muster enough courage to use nuclear arsenals for world supremacy. During Vietnam war more than fifty five thousand American soldiers were killed fighting the rebellions under Dr. Hochi Minh but USA's pentagon could not use their nuclear power. Recently in the Afghanistan and Iraq war, USA suffered humiliation and vast losses of men and material but could not dare to use its atomic power. It would not be incorrect to conclude that nuclear arsenals are meant only to showcase the might of the powerful nuclear nation and not to be used. The twentieth century has been a century of conflicts, with two world wars and also the dropping of atom bomb on Hiroshima and Nagasaki. The twenty first century in its infancy has become a century of terrorism and the use of human bombs. All these go on to further prove the futility of war. The old Marxian doctrine of inevibility of war has been replaced by the doctrine of coexistence in international politics. Hence both the capitalist and the communist power have been constrained to give up war as an option to settle their disputes. It means that war has lost its age old custom of settling disputes between one nation and another. Therefore we have to choose between atom and ahimsa. But as old habit die hard, we find it difficult to give up war easily. No doubt we have great craving for peace but still we go on preparing for war. More than thirty billion dollars are spent annually on manufacturing war materials in the world even when more than half of humanity languishes below poverty line with pathetic condition of education and health care facilities. Apart from creating an economic havoc there is a serious danger to our environment due to the fallout of atomic radiation. Hence it multiplies the dangers created by the industries, which has created ozone holes and produce acid rains. The accident in the nuclear plant at Chernobyl is a red signal to stop the threat of total genocide of mankind.

Dynamics of Peace

In the context of atomic age and unrestrained nuclear power all over the world, the concept of 'Global Peace' has become simply a matter of religious fad or some humanistic Utopia. Peace has become a categorical imperative for the existence of mankind. It has been a matter of moral and spiritual ideal from time immemorial but it has been willow-the-wisk till now. In spite of great emphasis on peace it has alluded our grasp. Hence we need to explore new horizons of peace. Peace requires new ideology and an ascetism and a new structure of our entire economic social and political system. We can't have peace in a world of plenty and poverty. Similarly world peace will remain a moon shine with autocratic and dictatorial rule. Like economic justice and social justice we should also have racial non-discrimination and religious non-fanaticisms for a peaceful world.

We shall discuss a few important points for establishing world peace.

***(a)* Universal Religion** : Almost all religions advocate and champion the cause of peace but the history of mankind has recorded nearly seven thousand small and big wars in the name of religion. Every religion thinks that it's the best which naturally implies that the rest of the religions are inferior. This is itself a potent cause for religious conflict, like imperialist powers every religion shows its imperialist design for expending its influence through propaganda and religious conversion. For example the two sects of Christianity, Catholics and the Protestant have fought hundred years of war amongst themselves. Similarly Islam and Christianity have been facing the 'clash of civilization' in modern times. Middle East has become the worst theatre of religious conflict. And even the Indian subcontinent has its share of religious fanaticism and obscurantism. Hence we need to change the structure of religion. Swami Vivekananda had said long ago that the days of personal and sectarian religions are over and we have to cultivate universal religion for universal peace. Tagore has also pleaded for the religion of man in place of religion of a sect. Raja Ram Mohan Roy had strongly pleaded for the spirit of universal religion to avoid nonsensical and endless religious conflict. Dr. Bhagwan Das in his magnum opus has held that there is an essential unity behind all religion. In short we can say that the days of personal and sectarian religion are over, they are not only outdated but also basically anti-human. Instead of binding together the entire humanity they have been instruments of disintegration, oppression and exploitation. Hence Marx was constrained to observe that 'Religion was the opium of masses' even Mahatma Gandhi advocated the concept of ethical religion.

(b) **Nationalism and World Peace :** When human being were facing dangers from unbridled tribalism and feudalism the cult of Patriotism came as a rescue and relief but soon nationalism degenerated into tribalism. During the entire course of human history over seven thousand wars have been fought in the name of patriotism and nationalism. Nationalism which had a progressive ideals of human civilization has lost its dynamics. Either we have a world government or world in chaos. In the ancient past Socrates said he was neither an Atheanian nor a Greek but a citizen of the world. In the ancient Vedic scriptures there is a mention of world fraternity. In modern times H.G. well, Bindal Wilkie, Bertrand Russell and others have pleaded for world government. In modern India Rahul Sanskritayan had also advocated the cause of world government in his book named 'Baiswi Sadi'. Even if we are able to achieve a formal semblance of world federation, we can cut down on unproductive defence expenditure and bring happiness to the world. In recent times twenty seven nations of western Europe have come under one umbrella, where there is one parliament, one common market, currency and visa provisions. Infact the United Nation had the greatest responsibility to usher in a world government but it has failed because it has become a chessboard of power politics. The U.S.A. has stolen the banner of U.N. and has created a number of organizations like the I.M.F., World Bank, W.T.O. etc for the exploitation of the developing nations. Only a world government with a world parliament and a world economy based on justice and equality can solve our problems.

(c) **Matriarchal System as the basis of World Peace :** During the last ten thousand years, the world has been under the oppressive and unjust patriarchal system, whether it is the political power or economics control or the religious authority, they have been brutally usurped by man in the patriarchal system of the society. Therefore Marx had rightly said that the first exploitation of mankind had begun by man upon women. Even Indian scriptures are full of gender discriminating injunctions and prohibition against women. Now it is high time to hand over the charge of the society and state to the matriarchal leadership. Since they have undergone immense sufferings and pain nurturing the human species. They are more likely to control the growing violence in social structure. A matriarchal order is less likely to be war prone and crime prone. Hence we can hope for a peaceful world.

The above recommendations for establishing world peace may sound too idealistic and much less practical but in the name of being practical, we have created a culture of vultures. Either we resolve for an honest disarmament or we have to choose between non-violence and non-existence. But the roots of violence are deeply entrenched in the very structure of our social fabrics. We need to make a start towards banishing violence from our inner self and only then we can try to abolish domestic violence, social and economic discrimination and political domination. Even in the field of education and sports, we have to eliminate the seeds of violence which emanates from the spirit called competition based on the faulty Darwinian doctrine of struggle for existence and survival of the fittest. Instead of competition, we have to develop a culture of co-operation and compassion. The spirit of competition has resulted in a vulgar display of wealth through a wrong principle development. Unless we hog a new Philosophy of human development based on voluntary poverty and simplicity, we would be compelled to foster an ecological disaster. Therefore Gandhi said "Nature had enough to meet our need but not our greed".

Index

C

O

P

Q